# FAMILY

## The Making & Remaking of a

# CHRISTIAN HOME

## ALSO BY RONALD HORTON

Mood Tides: Divine Purpose in the Rhythms of Life

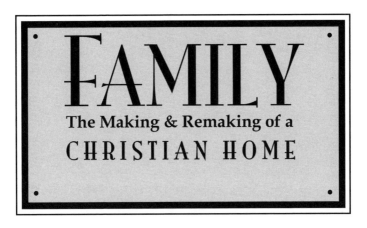

# FAMILY
## The Making & Remaking of a
## CHRISTIAN HOME

# Ronald Horton

journey**forth** ®

Greenville, South Carolina

**Library of Congress Cataloging-in Publication Data**
Horton, Ronald Arthur, 1936-
    Family : the making and remaking of a Christian home / Ronald
Horton.
        pages cm
    ISBN 978-1-60682-887-8 (perfect bound pbk. : alk. paper) —
ISBN 978-1-60682-888-5 (ebook) 1. Families—Religious aspects—
Christianity. 2. Families—Religious life. I. Title.
    BT707.7.H67 2014
    261.8'3585—dc23

                                                        2014007384

All Scripture is quoted from the King James Version unless otherwise
indicated.

NASB: Scripture from the New American Standard Bible, Copyright
© 1960, 1962, 1963, 1968, 1971, 1972, 1973, 1975, 1977, 1995 by
The Lockman Foundation. Used by permission.

Design by Nathan Hutcheon
Page layout by Michael Boone

© 2014 by BJU Press
Greenville, South Carolina 29614
JourneyForth Books is a division of BJU Press

Printed in the United States of America

ISBN 978-1-60682-887-8
eISBN 978-1-60682-888-5

15   14   13   12   11   10   9   8   7   6   5   4   3   2   1

*The mercy of the Lord is from everlasting to everlasting upon them that fear him, and his righteousness unto children's children.*

PSALM 103:17

*For my children*
*and their children*
*and all children*

# CONTENTS

# DIFFICULTIES

# DREAMS

# INTRODUCTION

# ANOTHER BOOK ON THE FAMILY?

This book would have been written had it never been offered for publication. It began as an adult Sunday School series on the family, on what holds families together and pulls them apart. I decided to put the lessons in writing to be passed on to my children and their children. But some who heard what I was up to or read portions of early drafts wanted it for their children as well. And so *Family: The Making and Remaking of a Christian Home* took shape over a number of years, finally appearing as the book you have in your hands today.

My interest in the subject sprang from a question I had long pondered. Isn't it interesting that side by side with the great pressing questions of apostolic times—salvation by grace through faith, Judaism and mysticism, church governance, Christ's return—the apostles Paul and Peter would have so much to say, and would say it with such earnestness, about the conduct of the family? Why might that be?

The immediate answer is that what happens in Christian families affects the life of the church. Churches are made up of families. Homes must be strong if the church is to thrive. Family leadership supplies church leadership: to qualify for their positions, pastors and deacons must be good leaders at home. The right functioning of the church depends on the right functioning of its families.

But that isn't all. God is interested in persons as persons, not just in persons as parts of groups. God's instructions for families in Scripture not only serve churches and families in the aggregate. They are life determining for individual Christians. They are meant for you and me. To flourish in a Christian family is to flourish in the kingdom of God.

In any case, what follows are some reflections from my own angle of vision on the cohesion of families. I have found in Scripture indications of what strengthens family connections. I have found also in Scripture indications of what strains these connections and opens dangerous rifts. I look back to my own formative years and find insights. My father speaks in his inimitable voice in these pages but also as a presence throughout.

Occasionally my half century of teaching will elbow its way in. My love of literature is part of what I am. But the book will have lost its way if it does not speak to the ordinary Christian, leaving a keener sense of what a home and a life given to God can be.

# FIRST THINGS

# CHAPTER 1

# THE OLD HOME PLACE

*Every man of the children of Israel shall pitch by his*
*own standard, with the ensign of his father's house.*
NUMBERS 2:2

When the Jews under Nehemiah began to rebuild the ruined wall of Jerusalem, they dug deep to find solid footing where the earlier wall had been. They meant to follow the line of that wall as far as they could before extending it outward. Doubtless they found the lower-level stones they were looking for. They also found other good stones scattered about that they could use in the visible parts of the wall. But their first challenge was dealing with the rubble. Daunting heaps of rubbish had to be dragged away before the work of building could begin.

When a young man and woman prepare for marriage, it is natural for them to cast appreciative but critical eyes on the homes they will be leaving. Their homes may be wonderfully exemplary. They may show years of attention to godly standards and goals, years in which love has reigned and spiritual values have mingled with practical judgment and good sense. Unfortunately, many Christian homes are not so. More and more it is the case that young persons from even highly regarded Christian families look back at their childhoods and see much rubble.

The family unit today is under attack as never before in modern memory. Satan has breached the walls of many a Christian home whose parents have struggled to maintain a godly order but have not entirely succeeded. Perhaps they did not struggle hard enough or long enough. They may have struggled but not altogether wisely. Their children, coming of age, may feel there is much to avoid in their parents' example. They may go so far as to repudiate their upbringing altogether. There is all that rubble.

Still the would-be homemakers may be uneasy, and rightly so, about making a clean break with their past. There is, after all, much to be desired in family continuity. God is pleased when children come to terms with their past, distinguish inherited strengths, and resolve to perpetuate in their own families His cumulative blessing. It does seem wise to determine the line of the existing walls and follow it as far as that line can reasonably go.

I am addressing at the outset what seems to me, humanly, the most important principle to be understood by young persons planning a home. Even before considering their options in building, they must understand the proper use of example. When children find glaring failures in their parents' examples, they may not be minded toward continuation. They may determine to build in a manner altogether different from that of their parents. They may in fact feel they need to scrap the entire edifice of their upbringing. They may even succeed in doing so, though escaping parental influence is more easily said than done.

Here is the point. Children need not accept indiscriminately the parental example they have inherited. That in fact could be a fatal mistake. But neither need they indiscriminately reject that example. In fact, they must not. Children are responsible to choose from their parents' example what is solid and worthy and to discard what is not. The responsibility for what they retain from that example and construct upon it is entirely their own, and the stakes are high.

In even the best of families, weaknesses mingle with strengths and mistakes can abound. The father may have deep godly convictions but weak emotional control; so did Moses. The mother may be too easily agitated by her fears and frustrations; so was Martha of Bethany. Discipline may be overdone or underdone.

Children may be overmanaged or undermanaged. Selfishness may lurk behind some family policies and decisions. Parental affection may be a flicker rather than a constant glow. Both parents may be disappointments to the children in numerous ways.

But it is an unusual home whose parental example is so deplorable that there are no positive elements for a child to approve and emulate. Jonathan knew very well the violent unstable nature of Saul, his father. Once at dinner Saul threw a spear at him to kill him. And yet Jonathan saw in his father a flawed greatness and never broke his filial bond. Son and father were inseparable, even in death (2 Sam. 1:23). Saul had been once a modest, self-effacing man (1 Sam. 15:17).

Even the worst of parents will in his better moments desire the best for his child and resolve to govern himself to warrant his child's trust. Wise children treasure such moments and keep those better qualities before them. They look for strengths within weakness. Worthy stones may lie about amidst all that rubble.

The psychological cost of rejecting even an unworthy parent can be high. Shakespeare's duke of Albany directs a stern warning to a rebel child.

> She that herself will sliver and disbranch
> From her material sap, perforce must wither
> And come to deadly use.
> (*King Lear*, 4.2.40–43)

A rebelling branch destroys itself; it may damage the tree.

The need for parental connection is deeply implanted in the human psyche. A child's rejection of his parents can be as debilitating to him as abandonment by his parents. To the pain of separation it adds the pain of guilt. But no less destructive than the active rejection of parents can be its passive form. Bitter defeatism, attributing failure in life to parental example, can be as dooming as an abrupt severing from one's parental stock. How can a child hope to succeed in life if he views his failures only as the result of others' wrongdoing? To take responsibility for what one is opens the way to positive change.

If parental example were all-determining, how could one account for the moral zigzag in the descendants of Uzziah on the throne of Judah? What could explain the succession of a Jotham by an Ahaz, of an Ahaz by a Hezekiah, of a Hezekiah by a Manasseh, of a Manasseh by a Josiah, of a Josiah by his wicked sons? The adage is not true that a child cannot rise above his upbringing—or sink below it too. From the same parents came a Cain, an Abel, and a Seth. Generational scapegoating shuts off hope.

In fact, Scripture places the main burden upon the child for how the child turns out. For every instruction given to parents, Scripture has many more for children. The godly grandfather, ungodly father, and godly son of Ezekiel 18 are singly responsible to God for what they are and what they do. Neither the righteousness nor the unrighteousness of the parent will be credited to the child. The child stands before God on his own spiritual footing. But that spiritual footing can include the best from his parents' characters and lives.

Personal accountability does not remove all blame from parents for their children's flaws. There is such a thing as overlapping responsibility. A caring parent does feel some responsibility for his child's shortcomings and may truly see his own faults imaged in his child's. But Scripture allows no room for self-exoneration on the part of children. No child need build on that part of his parents' example that he deplores. There is always the divine invitation to break a cycle of ungodly ancestry. "The Lord hath been displeased with your fathers. . . . Turn ye unto me . . . and I will turn unto you," said Israel's God through the prophet Zechariah (1:2–3). God's invitation to Israel is a promise of hope for a disappointed child.

A child honors his parents by perpetuating what is honorable in them. There is cumulative blessing when the strengths of even flawed parents flow into their children and a worthy line continues on.

# CHAPTER 2

# THE NEW HOME PLACE

*Hearken, O daughter, and consider, and incline thine*
*ear; forget also thine own people, and thy father's house.*
PSALM 45:10

Chapter 1 stressed the importance of maintaining parental connections. The new homemakers have much to learn from their elders in child raising, cooking, health, finances, and a host of other matters, large and small. There are years of insights to be tapped. The value of this experience may not register on the new husband and wife until they face situations requiring it. It is a foolish child who insists on acquiring all his knowledge first-hand. A welcoming spirit permits parental knowledge to cross generations.

That said, I must now qualify what I have been stressing at the risk of seeming to weaken it. Along with the appreciation of parental wisdom is a caution to be taken with equal seriousness. Parents of the newlyweds can be given too much say in the forming of the new home.

In Genesis, fundamental truths about human relationships appear in rudimentary form. After Adam has seen Eve for the first time, he exclaims, "This is now bone of my bones, and flesh of my flesh: she shall be called Woman, because she was taken out of Man." The application follows. "Therefore shall a man leave his father and mother, and shall cleave unto his wife: and they shall be one flesh" (Genesis 2:23–24). From the first recorded words of a human being we learn that a separation from one's father and mother is divinely intended in a marriage union.

As chapter 1 has I hope made clear, the leaving of parents does not mean a spurning of them. God expects children to follow the worthy ways of their predecessors. God authorizes ongoing parental authority in one regard. He says of Abraham, "For I know him that he will command his children and his household after him, and they shall keep the way of the Lord" (Gen. 18:19). But the primary loyalties of bride and groom must shift from their parents to each other. The new family is not meant to be a mere enlargement of the former ones.

This warning may seem to be challenged by the example of the patriarchs. Abraham and his children were nomads. In nomadic life, families cluster as clans. Clan authority flows from the elder members to the younger. By the time of Moses, the clans were associated in tribes headed by descendants of Jacob's sons. These patriarchal tribes became governing units in the national system. This hierarchical arrangement might seem to justify the incorporation of new families within the larger families from which they derive.

But Scripture does not support this model of the family as a universal pattern. In fact, what is striking in Genesis is the absence of interference by patriarchal heads in the families of their children and grandchildren. The autonomy of the family unit was assumed. When Jacob decided to leave his father-in-law, he conferred with his wives, not with their father. Though Laban claimed parental rights over his married daughters, the tone of the narrative does not support him. How remarkably this biblical example differs from the patriarchal model of some third-world cultures in which the bride is subjugated to her mother-in-law and the husband remains subject to his father and his father's father and so on. The final responsibility for the Israelite family was the father's and his alone.

It follows that when a parent because of age or disability or financial distress is taken into his child's family, his presence there does not affect the family order. The son or son-in-law remains the family head. This reversal of roles can be an awkward, painful business, but it must be clearly understood and accepted on both sides. The elder parent is now in a state of dependency and is under the rules of the household. If the family is conducted in a godly manner, he will be treated with all the deference and affection God expects of the young toward their elders. But the line of authority remains unchanged.

The situation becomes complex if a family is living in a grandparent's house. In such a case the grandparent retains the prerogatives of a landlord or a host. He can determine the use of his property. He can set the rules of house management as he would with other occupants. But he cannot preside over the home. He was not ceded family authority when his child's family moved in. Though the arrangement is sometimes necessary and can work beautifully with understanding on both sides, it is far from ideal.

The notion that elders retain a parental prerogative in their children's families is one of the most destructive mentalities that can intrude on a newly formed home. If a husband is more closely attached to his mother than to his wife, or the wife more attached to her father than to her husband, the family will be dangerously torn. The language of Genesis 2 is unambiguous: in marriage the man leaves his family and unites with his wife in a transfer of primary duty and affection. For the former bonds to stay paramount is a violation of a divine command.

It might have seemed perfectly reasonable, when my wife and I began marriage, for Martha, aged twenty-three to depend on her mother in all decisions of the home falling within her responsibility. Her mother, thirty-three years her senior, was more experienced in life and far more advanced in home skills. But the daughter was entitled to make her own way and find her own style. She knew to seek advice from her mother and did so, receiving it gratefully. But she also needed distance to make her own decisions and encouragement to shape her own home.

Fortunately her mother understood this need and tempered her involvement in the developing home.

When a husband keeps putting before his wife the example of his mother, he cruelly demoralizes her. When he maintains a warmer intimacy with his mother than with his wife, he demeans her, and his slight cuts to the core of their relationship. When a wife still looks to her father as the number-one man in her life, she does the same. Sons and mothers have a natural attachment to each other, as do daughters and fathers. There is no reason these special ties should ever cease to exist. But when they compete with those bonds uniting marriage partners, they violate Scripture and put the marriage in jeopardy. Cross-gender attachments of spouses to their parents, especially those binding husband and mother, are other than infidelity the most volatile disrupters of marriages and can be the most daunting obstacle for a marriage to overcome.

Newlyweds may need to assure a concerned mother of their openness to her suggestions while gently but firmly making it clear they alone must take responsibility for their new home and that family decision-making must go with it. They may need to decline financial help from an anxious father, explaining that it is better for the two of them to struggle a while, if need be, to make it on their own. Tactful distancing without rebuffing may require prayerful forethought and skill.

Couples planning marriage should try to understand the conflict of feelings within caring parents when their tenderly nurtured child is about to leave the home. The novelist Jane Austen provided an extreme example of the possessive type in the kind-hearted, worrying Mr. Woodhouse, widowed father of a lovely daughter nearing twenty-one. He lived alone with his daughter and hated to lose her. And so he could never be persuaded that marriages did anyone any good. For this simple, nervous man, "matches . . . are silly things, and break up one's family circle grievously" (*Emma*, vol. 1, chap. 1). He was won over with patience and intelligence and time.

# CHAPTER 3

# THE ABSENT MODEL

*God setteth the solitary in families.*

PSALM 68:6

In our study *family* has had the traditional sense of a married man and woman living together with their children, forming what is called a nuclear family. Scripture recognizes in addition to the nuclear family the augmented family, in which relatives such as grandparents live with the husband and wife and their children. It also recognizes the diminished family, in which one parent must carry the responsibility of two or in which the home is childless. Because of a husband's death, a family unit might consist of a widow and child (1 Kings 17:8–24) or, as in Naomi's case, a widow with daughters-in-law. A family might consist of only husband and wife, as did that of Zacharias and Elizabeth before they were blessed with a son, or for the duration of a childless marriage. Though the nuclear family will remain our paradigm, most of what is said of it can apply also to the augmented and diminished variations.

Since the nuclear model assumes monogamous marriage, it obviously cannot include polygamy. Though tolerated for a while in the Old Testament, polygamy brought family conflict and frustration and was never approved as normative. In the New Testament, polygamy is no option. The nuclear model also excludes unmarried cohabitation and communal-living arrangements like those of the hippies in the 1960s who practiced free love in defiance of traditional morality. Since the nuclear model unites gender opposites, it does not recognize homosexual unions, brazen mockeries of marriage, abhorrent to God.

Keeping in mind what Scripture means by a family, let us consider its importance. Here indeed is a problem. What is said in praise of the family and in the interests of strengthening it may seem cruelly to bypass victims of divorce and abandonment. The traditional nuclear family, once nearly universal in American society, is rapidly losing ground to the single-parent family. Women choose to have children without what seems to them the mere formality of marriage vows. Deadbeat dads and unmarried lovers acknowledge no responsibility toward the mother and child they have left behind. Abandoned children are left to the streets or to institutional care. Even members of traditional families may suffer abuse or neglect. Some turn to cults for a sense of belonging. How can what is said in support of the biblical family have meaning for them? How can it not be for them painfully excluding, a twisting of a knife in the heart? Our challenge then is to show the importance of the biblical family without making it all determining in the success of a life.

Evidence for the importance of well-ordered biblical families is all about us. Children from two-parent homes have a proven advantage in life, even by material standards. Few single mothers without help from relatives can provide a viable family income without a harmful loss of attention to their child. Along with material impoverishment is the loss of dignity from living on the public dole. Yet to have missed the benefits of a conventional family should not, for a Christian, be thought a doom.

It is striking how seldom in Scripture one encounters a normal home. Surely there must have been a number of such homes, but the spotlight does not fall upon many of them. Joseph's family was torn by strife, which eventually separated Joseph from his parents and brothers and cost him his youth. Moses was taken from his home as a baby and adopted into the family of Pharaoh. Samuel was given up by his mother to be raised by Eli, the priest.

The young David was taken from his family by Saul. The nameless maid in Naaman's household was separated from her family by captivity, as were young Daniel and his three friends. Esther had to be raised by her cousin.

A bountiful heavenly Father stands ready to make up the deficit in parental love and care for those deprived of a normal home. The psalmist has comfort for children deprived to the extreme. "When my father and my mother forsake me, then the Lord will take me up" (Ps. 27:10). Jesus said, concerning those separated from their families because of their devotion to Him, "There is no man that hath left house, or brethren, or sisters, or father, or wife, or children, or lands, for my sake, and the gospel's, but he shall receive an hundredfold now in this time, houses, and brethren, and sisters, and mothers, and children, and in the world to come eternal life" (Mark 10:29–30).

Jesus, addressing a contentious crowd, was told, "Thy mother and thy brethren stand without, desiring to speak with thee." He sharply replied, "Who is my mother? and who are my brethren?" He then "stretched forth his hand toward his disciples, and said, Behold my mother and my brethren. For whosoever shall do the will of my Father which is in heaven, the same is my brother, and sister, and mother" (Matt. 12:47–50). A major theme in the Lord's ministry is His welcoming of the marginalized into His family. They thrive once in.

We can speak of the huge importance of the traditional family as an institution established at the beginning by God. We can recognize it as the cornerstone of civil life and the best human guarantor of social stability. We can honor it as God's first means of moral and spiritual nurturing, of producing a "godly seed" (Mal. 2:15). We can read how God uses the relations of parent to child, of husband to wife, and of sibling to sibling to illustrate His relationship with His own earthly family, the church. And yet we can speak also of the unimportance of having had such a family. A Christian youth without a Christian home need not despair. God has not left him alone. His Heavenly Father, Elder Brother, and Great Companion are always there.

# CHAPTER 4

# OBEY THE RECIPE

*The word is very nigh unto thee . . .*
*that thou mayest do it.*
DEUTERONOMY 30:11–14

There is an advantage for young marrieds and soon-to-be-marrieds in having had good parental examples just as there is an advantage for a beginning homemaker in having had a mother who was a good cook. But to those without such examples I would offer the advice of my own favorite cook and home-maker of years past. If you are new to cooking and anxious about it, Martha would say, just obey the recipe. I would enlarge on her advice. If you are new to the grand art of home building and anxious about your readiness for the challenge, obey the recipe.

In his letter to the church at Colosse, a church he had never visited, Paul gave instructions about the makeup of a Christian home (Col. 3:18–21). The instructions are set out with elegant brevity. They suggest to my thinking that rare achievement of the human mind: a recipe in which the essentials are in simple order and unmistakably clear.

> Wives, submit yourselves unto your own husbands, as it is fit in the Lord.

> Husbands, love your wives, and be not bitter against them.

> Children, obey your parents in all things: for this is well pleasing unto the Lord.

> Fathers, provoke not your children to anger, lest they be discouraged.

Paul goes on to instruct slaves to obey their masters sincerely from the heart, and masters to treat their slaves with fairness. Many Roman households had slaves, and it is interesting that Paul treats them as parts of families with family obligations and needs. These instructions to masters and slaves will not concern us here apart from the passing observation that justice and fairness and cheerful obedience affect the happiness of the Christian home.

We will have occasion in the following pages to elaborate on this inspired model of the family. But it is a point to be emphasized here how succinctly the model can be stated. Virtually all family troubles are due to deviations from Paul's instructions in Colossians 3.

# NEXT THINGS

# CHAPTER 5

# THE NEW KINSHIP

*This is now bone of my bones, and flesh of my flesh.*
GENESIS 2:23

The family is the first human institution ordained of God, and it receives instant attention in Scripture. The relationship of husband and wife is explained immediately after Eve's creation (Gen. 2:18–24). The effects of sin on this relationship are explained immediately after the fall (Gen. 3:16). What we need most to know about the family is condensed in these passages.

From Genesis 2:23–24 we learn the constitutive power of the marriage union. It produces a *new kinship*. This kinship is equal, indeed superior, to existing family relationships. Two from separate blood lines (after Adam) come together as "one flesh," composing a new line of descent. It will not do for one spouse to say to the other, "Well, blood is thicker than water. My daddy and mama brought me into the world. I met you at Walmart." Blood may be thicker than water, but it is not as substantial as flesh.

This new kinship, as noted in Chapter 2, is an *independent relationship*. It amounts to a new bond, a new loyalty that has precedence over the existing loyalties of kinship. The duty remains to honor parents and provide for them when they cannot provide for themselves (Mark 7:9–13). But the tectonic plates have shifted. A new landmass has split off the old. "For this cause [marriage] shall a man leave his father and his mother." The new family is not a promontory on the previous one.

From the same passage we learn that this independent relationship is also an *intense and enduring relationship.* The man will "cleave unto his wife" and she to him. "Cleave" depicts the intensity of the relationship. It is fervently maintained. "Cleave" also indicates the persistency of the new relationship. Marriage is a three-way contract. God is party to it. A contract cannot be broken without the consent of all the parties. Unless, that is, one of them brings suit. Obviously God is not subject to civil litigation.

It follows that this kinship is an *inviolable relationship.* Since God is a party in the three-way contract, an attempt by a fourth party to interfere with the contract incurs God's stern disapproval and serious judicial consequences. The Thessalonians were praised by Paul for their eager embrace of the gospel and their energetic efforts to spread it. But in Thessalonica, as in other Gentile cities, the gospel had to make its way within a licentious moral environment. Paul warns the Christians there about sexual promiscuity.

> This is the will of God, even your sanctification, that ye should abstain from fornication: that every one of you should know how to possess his vessel in sanctification and honour, not in the lust of concupiscence, even as the Gentiles which know not God; that no man go beyond and defraud his brother in any matter, because that the Lord is the avenger of all such, as we also have forewarned you and testified. (1 Thess. 4:3–6)

Fornication with a Christian brother's spouse is a theft. It deprives him of what he possesses by solemn contract. Since as a theft it most likely involves deceit, it is also a fraud. Paul writes that God, the third party in the contract, will not be deceived and will take the side of the deceived party, avenging his loss. The adulterer should understand that in despising his brother and his brother's exclusive right to his spouse, he is also despising God (1 Thess. 4:8).

When Jesus cited Genesis 2:23 on the absoluteness of the marriage contract, the disciples were staggered by His words. They seem to have doubted whether the relationship as described was achievable. "If the case of the man be so with his wife, it is not good to marry" (Matt. 19:10). They realized the height of this standard, and Jesus agreed with them. He mentioned three kinds of persons who from reason or necessity remain unmarried: those who are born incapable of marriage or disposed toward celibacy ("so born from their mother's womb"), those rendered physically incapable of marriage by human action ("made eunuchs of men"), and those who have foregone marriage "for the kingdom of heaven's sake" (Matt. 19:12).

Paul is an example of the last category, one who had decided against marriage as an encumbrance to his life as a pioneer missionary marked for persecution. But marriage was to be respected by all as a divine uniting of hearts, minds, and bodies, a union ratified, enforced, and defended by God. A natural response to the biblical view of marriage is that of Jesus' disciples—amazement and absolute awe.

# CHAPTER 6

# WHO SERVES?

*I have given unto you an example,*
*that ye should do as I have done to you.*
JOHN 13:15

After Eve and Adam sinned and sin entered the bloodstream of the human race, it might seem that God's purposes for His chief creation were forever frustrated. But God set about quickly to contain the damage. Judicial consequences followed for Satan, Eve, and Adam. Adam was placed in the garden to dress it. Now he will farm. His labor will be for his subsistence and will be exhausting. He must now till a soil that has been cursed. He must "eat his bread," provide his living, "by the sweat of [his] face" (Gen. 3:19). Eve will suffer in child bearing. She also will relate to Adam in a less agreeable way. Eve was created as a help for Adam. She will still be that, but her help to Adam will be subservient.

Adam will serve his work. What Adam did pleasantly with cooperative soil—it was a God-prepared garden—will now be done with difficulty. Eve will serve her husband. What she knew as a joyous and free relationship will now be a subjugation. This is not to say any virtue accrues to a spouse in making these judgments more burdening than they need be. Shunning technological improvements in farming or abjuring anesthesia in childbirth does not raise one's estimation with God, though these choices might be made for good reasons. To be overbearing toward his wife does not make a husband a co-worker with God. But the curses on Adam and Eve would bring new challenges.

Among these challenges were new psychological needs. There is psychological value in work. It is a human fact that work can be pleasurable, not onerous. Beyond that, a routine of work is an emotional regulator. An early retiree may discover that the steady load on his body and mind imposed by the work he has escaped acted as a balance wheel, keeping his psychic machinery running smoothly. An inability to work may require emotional coping.

The same is true of a wife's service to her husband and family. Her labors can be immensely satisfying—such that she would not be deprived of. Her desire toward her husband, her self-fashioning according to his need for her, can be fulfilling rather than degrading. God's curse on the human pair was to entwine pain with their good. To understand this truth is as important as anything can be to a winsome view of the biblical marriage union.

It is obvious that what we have read from Paul in Colossians 3:18–21 aligns with what God tells Eve about her rule by her husband. Paul's first command, that wives submit to their husbands, clearly gives the rule of the family to the father. The reason is not just punitive. Authority is given for the purpose of carrying out obligation. Its scope equals that of the obligation it exists to perform. Since the father is answerable to God for the good of the family, he must be granted the freedom to enact it. The selfish use of authority is a perversion of the concept and an abuse of power.

The third command gives husband and wife the rule of their children. This rule not only maintains family peace but is profoundly important for the well-being of the children. Benefits flow to the child content to be served by his parents. These benefits extend far beyond the present. There is no escaping the truth that the child in later life will always be answerable to someone on whom his good depends. One of the greatest benefits parents can give their child is the ability to situate himself cheerfully under authority. It can be inferred that the first and third commands of Paul not only give authority to husbands and parents but also in effect *require it of them*. The good of the entire family, including their own good as parents, depends upon the conscientious performance of their indicated duties.

What is being described in Colossians 3 is a benign hierarchy, a structure of strength and beauty, vastly satisfying as all perform their roles. Family authority has nothing to do with intrinsic worth. The woman is not naturally inferior to the man, nor are children to their parents. All have dignities to be respected. The subordination of the wife to her husband and of the children to their parents is a positional inferiority required for the well-functioning of the home. Whether he wants to or not, the man must rule. Whether she finds it agreeable or not, the woman must situate herself under his leadership. Whether the parents feel up to it, they must require obedience of their children. Whether the children have agreeable parents, they must obey. The only qualification Paul adds to the requirement of obedience in these instances is the universal one—that it be "in the Lord" (Eph. 6:1; Col. 3:18).

The command of obedience toward parents rather than just toward the father makes clear that the woman's role in family management is one of co-rule. The family, absent the father, is not subject to the eldest adult son, as in some cultures, but to the mother. "Ye shall fear every man his mother, and his father," said the Lord in Leviticus 19:3. The mother is the home keeper, or home manager, under her husband's direction. If the husband is thoughtful, he will bring himself under her management in household business rather than exempt himself from the duties he has delegated to her.

It is interesting that Paul chooses a different Greek word to express the woman's responsibility to her husband from the word expressing children's responsibility to parents. The word translated "submit unto" in the command to wives is not the same word translated "obey" in the command to children. It connotes the arranging oneself, as in the military, under a positional superior. The same differentiation between the duties of children and wives occurs in a parallel passage in Ephesians, where children are told to obey their parents and wives to submit to their husbands. In the verse that precedes the Ephesians passage, all believers are to be "submitting yourselves one to another in the fear of God" (Eph. 5:21). What is evidently intended here is not a mere "Yes, Sir" response to snapped commands but the situating of oneself serviceably in a subordinate role.

Paul has more to say on the subject in two other epistles. Titus 2:5 has been misread to require wives to stay at home. The expression "keepers at home" in King James English refers to home-keeping, home management, home governance. Wives are to take charge of the home. In 1 Timothy 5:14, Paul expresses his will that the younger widows "marry, bear children, guide the house," rather than wander about idly. Clearly he is designating a sphere of responsibility with the authority to go with it that elevates the woman in the family order. This sphere can extend as far as her desires and abilities permit. She is in basic ways the center of the home, her husband being the head; and a special dignity attends on her position. The psalmist depicts the wife in a God-blessed home as an encircling "fruitful vine" nurturing the household (Ps. 128:3). Her status in Scripture is high.

What Paul specifies for rule of the family is a top-down authority structure but not a despotism. Children are subordinate to parents and the mother is subordinate to the father, but the father has his superior too. "The head of the woman is the man," but "the head of every man is Christ" (1 Cor. 11:3). David the shepherd-king tells his family and his kingdom in Psalm 23 that "the Lord is *my* shepherd." The shepherd needs a shepherd, and has a divine one. The Christian family then is not an autocracy but a theocracy. In view of its benefits, it is a commonwealth under God.

That the head of the family has obligations downward is clear from Colossians 3, which provided our recipe. It is notable that two of the four injunctions concerning obedience are given to the father. Husbands are to love their wives and not be harsh (the KJV meaning of "bitter") toward them (Col. 3:19). It is a neglected fact that the traditional marriage vows can be broken in more than one way. They can be broken by the failure to forsake all others. But they can also be broken by a failure to love, honor, and cherish. "Cursed be the man that obeyeth not the words of his covenant," preached Jeremiah (11:2–3). God's stern disapproval rests on all breakers of sacred vows.

Fathers are here instructed not to provoke their children to anger (Col. 3:21). "O Lord, correct me, but with judgment; not in thine anger, lest thou bring me to nothing," prays Jeremiah on behalf of sinning Israel (Jer. 10:24). Paul, in another context, warns inconsiderate Christians to "destroy not the work of God" (Rom. 14:20). It is one thing to subdue a child's will in his own interests, that is, in order to make him responsive to necessary instruction. It is quite another to break his spirit by wrathful tirades and unreasonable restrictions, behaviors less likely to weaken a child's will than to stiffen it.

An angry father produces an angry son. "Make no friendship with an angry man; and with a furious man thou shalt not go: lest thou learn his ways, and get a snare to thy soul" (Prov. 22:24–25). A furious, berating father may lose his child's heart and his wife's as well. A mother confident of her husband's emotional control will less likely feel compelled to interfere in his correction of their children.

It is the father's responsibility to rule his family in a loving, considerate way while maintaining the necessary firmness. He leads in sacrifice. He asks more of himself than of his family. He leads in love. He is energetic in generosity, delighted to provide those extras he knows will please his family as he is able and to the extent he can.

He also leads in sensitivity. A wife needs continuing reassurance of her husband's love and of his appreciation of her role. Children need continuing reassurance of their parents' love and of their own importance in the family. The father leads as a provider of the physical and emotional needs of the family but also of its spiritual needs, situating his wife and children agreeably in a church where they can spiritually grow and be blessed. Wise fathers are sensitive to these needs and endeavor to satisfy them.

In the family order described by Paul, who then serves? The children serve upwardly. They are charged with obedience to their parents. They must serve their parents if their parents are to serve them. The wife serves both upwardly and downwardly. She is charged with submission to her husband and with the care of her household. The father, the earthly head of the family, serves upwardly his divine Head and reports to Him directly. But he also serves downwardly. He serves his wife and children and the family in aggregate. He is charged with their well-being.

His obligation rests mightily on his shoulders. It includes more than his family's subsistence. He is its giver-in-chief. To serve his family as he should he will need to join with his mate in seeking the help of the greatest Servant of all.

That great Servant put the question of service and status bluntly to His disciples, who from their behavior to one another needed to ponder it. "Whether is greater, he that sitteth at meat, or he that serveth? Is not he that sitteth at meat? But I am among you as he that serveth" (Luke 22:27). Jesus shamed them by washing their feet, a lowly task they would not have considered doing for one another. To resist service for the sake of status is to resist the example of God.

Shakespeare's last play, the last written entirely by himself, is often thought to have been his farewell to his vocation. The great dramatist appears to have written himself into the play as the exiled duke Prospero, cast adrift on a bewitched isle, with only his magic books and young daughter to sustain him. He takes control of the island and turns his attention to his daughter. Miranda is approaching marriageable age without a worthy suitor, or any suitor.

Prospero learns of a royal flotilla passing within reach of his magic and contrives to bring about a shipwreck tossing the royal party on the shore. Included among the nobles is young Ferdinand, heir to the throne, a youth of exceptional character and beauty. Prospero sees in Ferdinand a potential husband for

Miranda and enslaves him, subjecting him to a test. Ferdinand must carry firewood to Prospero's cave—a task unfit for any nobleman.

For Ferdinand the work is not at all burdensome since it allows him to be with Miranda. Miranda wants to help him carry the wood, but he will hear none of it.

*Miranda.*                  If you'll sit down,
I'll bear your logs the while. Pray give me that,
I'll carry it to the pile.

*Ferdinand.*             No, precious creature,
I had rather crack my sinews, break my back,
Than you should such dishonor undergo,
While I sit lazy by . . .
                       Hear my soul speak:
The very instant that I saw you, did
My heart fly to your service, there resides,
To make me slave to it, and for your sake
Am I this patient log-man.

Miranda's father has been watching unseen from a distance.

*Prospero*           Fair encounter
Of two most rare affections! Heavens rain grace
On that which breeds between 'em.

The pace of their love is too slow for Miranda. She is overcome.

*Miranda*          Hence, bashful cunning,
And prompt me, plain and holy innocence!
I am your wife, if you will marry me;
If not, I'll die your maid. To be your fellow
You may deny me, but I'll be your servant,
Whether you will or not.

How does Ferdinand respond? As a real man would.

*Ferdinand*         My mistress, dearest,
And I thus humble ever.

Then Miranda.

*Miranda*     My husband then?

Then Ferdinand.

*Ferdinand*    Ay, with a heart as willing
As bondage e'er of freedom.

(Tempest 3.1.60–88)

Did ever lovers, in literature or in life, more ache to serve each other?

# CHAPTER 7

# SUBORDINATION OR MUTUALITY?

*Yet is she thy companion.*
MALACHI 2:14

It is understandably small comfort to a woman to be assured she is a valued underling in the family order. That would be a grossly inadequate description of the relationship she believes she has or ought to have with her husband. The Bible has too often been used for male advantage in a cruelly condescending way.

In Malachi 2, God's rebuke of heartless husbands divorcing their wives speaks to the right of wives to be valued as persons, not as disposable chattel. "Yet is she thy companion, and the wife of thy covenant" (Mal. 2:14). God recalls His purpose in the marriage union: "And did He not make one?" (2:15). The language of Genesis makes clear that the Creator intended a union of two distinct natures. "God created man in his own image, in the image of God created he him; male and female created he them" (Gen. 1:27). Both natures would come together in the fullest human expression of who He is. Human nature in its completest form was gendered from the beginning.

The language of Scripture speaks of a richer, profounder relationship than can be expressed in stern hierarchical terms. It does more than assign contracting parties their parts in a hierarchy. It sets them on a path to be traveled together as long as both live. Yes, the one will lead and the other will follow, but they will at the same time be traveling in step, sharing thoughts and purposes, exchanging comfort, serving each other's interests and needs (1 Cor. 7:3–4). The woman sees herself and is seen by her husband as not just the dutiful occupant of a hierarchical niche but as his devoted companion and friend.

So can the hierarchical model of the marriage relationship survive this description? Or should it be displaced by a companionate model? To put the question in school-grammar terms, is marriage a subordinating or coordinating conjunction? When two ideas seem to oppose each other in Scripture, it will not do to choose one and dispense with the other. The two may coexist in a complementary way. Let's return now to the hierarchical idea of the family underlying Paul's instructions in Colossians 3 and see how it may coexist with the idea of marriage as a union of equals.

First, recall that in the biblical account ranked authority exists not for its own sake but for a positive purpose. In 1 Corinthians, Paul speaks of differences of administration in the church and of persons gifted accordingly. All functions are important, and all persons perform those for which they are suited for the good of the whole. No one is lessened by occupying a less prominent place in the church. "Can the eye say to the hand I have no need of you, or the head to the feet I have no need of you?" (1 Cor. 12:21). In fact, says Paul, continuing his analogy with the body, the less eminent parts are given "the more abundant honour" (1 Cor. 12:23). The less conspicuously placed members of the congregation are to understand the excellence of their roles. In his first Epistle Peter enjoins husbands, concerning their wives, to "dwell with them according to knowledge, giving honour as unto the weaker vessel, and as being heirs together of the grace of life" (1 Peter 3:7).

It is a truth never to be forgotten that there is more to what we are and amount to in the divine accounts of church and family than the particular positions we happen to hold. Each of us has someone over us and under us in God's vast patriarchy, but we stand as equals in the household of faith. As in the Godhead there is voluntary subordination of the Son to the Father with co-equality, so in a marriage the wife situates herself voluntarily and in love beneath the one who is given her as her head, and she does so with no diminishment in honor and worth. The dignity of the desired woman, the sense of her value to her lover and her value to herself, is unmistakable in Solomon's Songs.

Looked at in this way, every duty performed for the Lord has a splendor about it. It can also be personally satisfying. A woman who has come to love her nurturing, guiding role in the family may be impatient with what interferes with it. She may feel liberated when the main burden of family rule is settled on her husband, allowing her immersion in what she feels is most central to her and what she most enjoys. It is not unknown for leaders to wish to downsize their public responsibilities. Many a pastor would love to be freed from the mechanics of church administration to have more time for pulpit preparation and pastoring his people. There is broad symbolism in Shakespeare when a new king marvels at the weight of the crown and envies the freedom of his subjects. Plato's philosopher-kings are forced to rule when they prefer instead their private lives.

If there is a greater honor than to be given a superior place, it is to be honored, like Mordecai, by one's superior. The good woman of Proverbs 31 is praised by her husband as well as by her children and the community. "Her children arise up, and call her blessed; her husband also, and he praiseth her. . . . Give her of the fruit of her hands, and let her own works praise her in the gates" (Prov. 31:28–31). Her works are her family, and she is praised by them. She seems not to have been envious of her husband's position in the family order. Nor should she have been. The Bible does not contain a chapter-length tribute to a virtuous husband.

We learn from the same chapter in Proverbs that the woman so extolled by her family and community was more than a stay-at-home mom in the strictest use of that expression. Yes, she performed her home duties with energy and style, but that was not all. Her home duties took her beyond her home. She engaged the commercial world to provide for her family (Prov. 31:14). She opened her heart to the poor (Prov. 31:20). She was something of a business woman, buying land and conducting trade (Prov. 31:16, 24), initiatives normally thought of as belonging to a husband. She was no shrinking violet. While undertaking ventures on behalf of her family she was enlarging her personal world.

She is not the only enterprising woman in the Bible. The "great woman" of Shunem in 2 Kings 4 acted for her family in extending hospitality to Elisha. Whenever he came to her village, she "constrained him to eat bread" (4:8). She spoke to her husband about providing the prophet a room to stay in when he passed by, and so they did. In the events of chapters 4 and 8 pertaining to the Shunemite family—the promise of a child, its birth and death and restoration to life, the restoration of stolen land—it is the woman rather than her husband who is the consequential figure in the story.

It was the woman, not the man, of the house with whom the prophet must deal, and he did so with respect and sensitivity. She brought Elisha within her care and devised a plan to serve him in a more substantial way than he was used to. When her child died, it was she who rode to the prophet to insist on his help. When a famine was coming, it was she Elisha told to take her family and leave the land, and she did. Nothing in the story suggests disapproval of her forwardness.

Luke's narrative in Acts shows strong women helping the spread of the gospel, but also strong women resisting its spread. We learn of Lydia, a business woman, a "seller of purple," who served Paul as the Shunemite did Elisha, "constraining" Paul and Luke to stay with her in her ample house at Philippi (Acts 16:14–15). We read of Phoebe carrying the letter of Paul to Rome from Corinth. We are told of Priscilla, along with her husband, Aquila, mentoring Apollos. Not only in Philippi but also in Thessalonica and Berea the gospel was received by "chief" or "honourable" women "not a few" (Acts 17:4, 12). At Antioch of

Pisidia the Jews stirred up "the devout and honourable women" along with "the chief men of the city" to drive Paul and Barnabas from the town.

Women in the Roman world were not necessarily the abject, powerless creatures they are sometimes thought to have been. From the imperial court down, women swayed decisions and had influence and prestige. Nor were Christian women held in disregard. Eight of the twenty-six singled out by Paul for special greeting in Romans 16 are women. One of them, mother of Rufus, Paul refers to affectionately as "his mother and mine" (Rom. 16:13). The women were likely acting in concert with their husbands, if they were married, or with their husbands' consent. But they acted with purpose and conviction and were approved for doing so.

There may come a time in a marriage, in even the best of marriages, when a wife must momentarily take the lead from her husband—when he is shaken, when he requires steadying, when he has need of comforting words to draw him back from dejection or stiffening words to call him to his duty. He may need to be taken by the lapels, as it were, in chastening rebuke: "Where is that man I married, the man that sought the Lord and faced down those difficulties back then, and with the Lord's help got us through?" Let it never be said that a wife's courage and steel of character should not come to the fore at such times. Blessed is the man who has a woman of tenderness and resolve by his side.

A wife has a twofold challenge, especially to a man with strong views. She is subject to his leadership. But she is also his best friend, and she has the prerogatives of a best friend. One of those prerogatives is to tell him what he needs to know when no one else will do it. She is supportive of her husband but she also balances him. She does not, like Esther before Xerxes, enter his throne room with fear. She lives secure in his presence and he in hers. If she feels she has to tiptoe around his ego, Xerxes needs to grow up. He isn't half enough a man.

It follows that a first question for serious couples to get settled is whether they are educable—whether each is willing to learn from the other. A failure on this point bodes ill for the happiness of a marriage. Everyone needs an adoring critic, and who is better suited for this role than a spouse? To have such a one is to be signally blessed of God.

# CHAPTER 8

# TYRANTS AND TRUANTS

*Withhold not correction from the child.*
PROVERBS 23:13

After Adam and Eve were expelled from the garden, God gave them a son and then another son. The elder of the two killed his brother, evidently from envy. Cain's parents must have wondered in their grief what they could have done differently and what might be left for them to do now. We have no way of knowing what God had taught Adam and Eve about child raising. We do know that Satan has a way of garbling God's instructions so we only half know what we once knew and ought still to know.

Cain may have missed a general truth affecting all of life. This truth is a master theme in Scripture. It is also assumed in some great literature of the past, the plays of Shakespeare, for example. Today's progressive thinkers find it insufferable, for it jars with their radical assumptions. But the wise of all generations have understood its importance to the safety and health of their nations. I refer to the necessity of subordination to human happiness.

Society in the Western world was at one time legally hierarchical, and it was understood that public order could be breached in two ways. It could be breached if subjects refused to obey. This was the more immediate and visible cause of disorder.

It could also be breached if rulers failed to rule—to rule, that is, as they should. Of the two causes of civil breakdown, the latter, the failure to rule, was the deeper and posed the greater danger. A ruler's failure to rule would incite his subjects to rebel. It was an axiom that trouble in the kingdom begins with trouble in the king.

Subjects of kings were thought to be moved to obedience by two demeanors of their ruler. A show of majestic sternness coupled with a readiness to punish wrong would produce fear. A kindness toward subjects, a willingness to bend an ear to their complaints and show them friendship, would induce love. The two needed to exist together. Severity without friendship would raise anger. Friendship without severity would prompt wickedness. Support for these observations was found in the history of Israel, when for example the kingdom was split because of Rehoboam's blunt rejection of the people's request for kind treatment.

A lack of these demeanors was dangerous to civil order. A king could jeopardize his peace and the peace of his kingdom by ruling harshly. Worse, he could almost ensure his downfall by preferring not to rule. Preferring not to rule could take two forms. A king could formally abdicate, retiring prematurely. Or he could informally abdicate by slackness. That is, he could in effect abandon his rule by simply going through the motions of his office and trusting the conduct of his realm to ambitious underlings. Maintaining order was always an uneasy business. Kingdoms might fall through either the tyranny or the truancy of a king.

These venerable truisms are worth the space given them here because of their parallels in the rule God has ordained for the family. The family head must not be a tyrant. Husbands must love their wives and not be "bitter against them [that is, harsh toward them]" (Col. 3:19). Fathers must not provoke their children to wrath (Col. 3:21). A child oppressed by a cruel father may reject all authority. "The wrath of man worketh not the righteousness of God" (James 1:20). A woman treated unkindly by a domineering husband cannot easily model the cheerful submission both parents expect of their children. Children as well as mothers have a sense of what is just. They recognize favoritism and capricious rule. They take note of angry outbursts and disdain.

The cruelty of a tyrant father will cost him personally. He has ruled by fear without love. Now his grown children are out of the home, if they haven't left before, and are past intimidating. What does he have left from them? Long before he lost their obedience, he lost their love. His wife was never his companion. Now he is alone.

A truant father may be even more pitiable, and for this reason. Children have been known to forgive cruelty. They rarely forgive neglect. Here is Dad, home from work, quite willing to leave family rule to his exhausted wife. He sinks into a chair to watch the news while she labors over dinner, struggling to control the children and also herself. Dad is deaf to the news of the day that most matters, that of the family. The children cluster around their mother, if they are not running about testing her patience. Dad is pathetically detached. There is more than one kind of single-parent family. There is more than one definition of a deadbeat dad.

The Bible gives two notable examples of fatherly detachment, both prominent men of God. Eli, the high priest, had two sons, "men of Belial," who "knew not the Lord." They "abhorred the offering of the Lord," seizing their priestly shares of the offerings in disregard of the Mosaic stipulations. They even committed fornication with the women who congregated at the door of the tabernacle. Judgment came on them and on their father because they "made themselves vile, and he restrained them not" (1 Sam. 2:12; 3:13). God's voice was fierce toward the father: Wherefore "honourest [thou] thy sons above me?" (1 Sam. 2:29).

The king of Israel most celebrated in Scripture was a truant also. Of Adonijah, David's eldest son, who tried to seize the throne ahead of Solomon, the chronicler observes, "His father had not displeased him at any time in saying, Why hast thou done so?" (1 Kings 1:6). David's earlier failure to rule his family had born bitter fruit in the revolt and subsequent death of Absalom, a crushing grief to his father. Both Absalom and Adonijah, like Eli's two sons, died miserable deaths. Their actions also brought division and suffering on the nation.

The Bible is mostly silent on the responsibility of parents for how their child turns out except in the one matter of moral nurturing—their duty to command, teach, and reprove him. Sadly, there are parents who love their children, they think, too much to correct them—a foolish love, if a love at all. They cannot bring themselves to put their child to any pain. There is the child's dignity to be considered. Or so they justify their reluctance to take direct action. At bottom is the real cause—a fear of losing their child's love.

They should have a greater fear. Grave consequences loom for the undisciplined child. He may become a lifelong misfit and wonder why. He may wonder why he cannot tell himself what to do and follow through with it. He may be helpless to defeat an addiction. It is a child to be pitied who has never had the benefit of wisely administered parental pain. He will have to cope as best he can with the far-greater pain in life he might have avoided. Years ago I heard a psychiatrist remark that if life never offered occasions to say no to a child, it would be necessary to invent them. Otherwise, the child would enter life without "frustration muscles." By being governed by others we learn to govern ourselves.

Beyond worldly success is what matters for both time and eternity. The goodly life in the fullest sense is the God-blessed life, a life conducted in obedience to God. The father's role is consequential here. From his father the son gets his first impressions of God. It is true that by the fear of God Scripture means more than just abject terror, but we mustn't exclude from the expression that very real fear of the consequences of doing wrong. Paul wrote, "Knowing the terror of the Lord I persuade men," referring most likely to his experience on the road to Damascus (2 Cor. 5:11). The apostle spoke of both "the goodness and severity of God" (Rom. 11:22). If a child has little fear of his father, he will likely be deficient in that fear of God referred to in Scripture as "the beginning of wisdom" (Ps. 111:10). A child naturally picks up the fears he observes in his parents. Among those fears is that wholesome and necessary one, the fear of the Lord. But above all motivations for family discipline, beyond even the good of the child, is the father's own primary concern, his sense of personal obligation to God. Having children "in all subjection" is something he as the under-head of the family owes to the family's Supreme Head (1 Tim. 3:4). He is acting on God's behalf in God's cause, the well-being of those he leads. The weight of his responsibility, once understood, should inspire the compliance of his family.

# DIFFICULTIES

# CHAPTER 9

# PUSH AND PULL

*Above all things, have fervent charity among yourselves;*
*for charity shall cover the multitude of sins.*

1 PETER 4:8

A dam's yielding to Eve has been considered by theologians the paramount instance of truancy on the part of a husband. Adam vacated his role as her head to follow her in an act of dishonor, an act with far-reaching consequences. Afterward, Eve, in John Milton's epic treatment of the subject, says in essence, "Then, why didn't you stop me?" Milton's Eve was at fault, but Adam, the more knowledgeable, had the greater blame because he deliberately followed her into sin. Certainly on both sides, in the taking of the fruit by Eve and in the receiving of the fruit from Eve by Adam, there was a notable breakdown in the family order, costing the original pair and their posterity the happiness God had intended for them in the garden.

A wife able to overbear her husband's will in small matters should fear she can do so in weighty matters, matters that concern her good and the larger good of the family. When God appoints a man to leadership, He can be expected to communicate to him insights He may not care to share with those he leads. A father's views are not to be considered infallible, but they carry a presumptive legitimacy not guaranteed to the rest of the family.

An overbearing wife should consider the cost to her family of always getting her own way.

She should also consider the cost to herself. There is such a thing as a woman's not being content until she can dominate her husband, and then later realizing she cannot respect a man she can dominate. If a wife wishes to be married to a man who doubts his capacities and his worth, she can question them until he agrees they are very little indeed and he is reduced to a size both can despise.

She will share in the loss. Her stature has shrunk along with his. If her husband is not worth much, why then did she choose him? If she thinks so poorly of him, what is left of her wifehood for anyone to admire? Her children will have noticed. They will have learned that their father does not deserve their honor, and that neither does she.

The paternal honor she has stripped from her husband has not transferred to her. Children learn respect for their parents from their parents' respect for each other. If the mother will not accept the leadership of the father, it is unlikely the children will accept either's leadership. The mother will receive back from her children the same behavior she has shown their father. She will hear from them the same words, as if played back on a tape, which she has directed toward him.

"Every wise woman buildeth her house, but the foolish plucketh it down with her hands." So says the wise man of Proverbs 14:1. It is not just marital infidelity that destroys families. The slow erosion of family order is equally deadly, though in a less dramatic way. A demoralized husband can give up on family leadership. He can withdraw from his duties, and also from the family fellowship—a situation fraught with danger for everyone. When frustration builds over time, when more and more in the apostle's words railing is rendered for railing (1 Peter 3:9), a point of exhaustion can be reached at which a husband no longer cares. A study conducted by the National Institute of Mental Health "found that the single most important prediction of divorce was the husband's being withdrawn and disappointed"

(*Omni,* December, 1993, 38). Shakespeare's Rosalind has stern advice for proud Phoebe, belittler of her simple shepherd lover Silvius. "Down on your knees and thank heaven fasting for a good man's love" (*As You Like It,* 3.5.57–58).

But the aggressive wife may be a neglected wife. The husband may think his home less interesting than his work. He may be obsessed with material success. "He that is greedy of gain troubleth his own house" (Prov. 15:27). He may be emotionally detached by nature and disinclined to change. If his own parents contained their feelings and if his own temperament tends that way, factors often occurring together, expressions of affection may not come easily to him, and he may not think it worth his while to try to change. A normal good marriage will enrich a life beyond imagination; but it will also constrain a life beyond imagination, that is, beyond the imagination of a self-occupied man. A wife who feels herself neglected by her husband can seek his attention by contesting his domain.

A husband may neglect his wife for less selfish reasons. He may allow his work to override his attention to her and the children as being, he supposes, more necessary to the family's well-being. If so, he has failed to understand the importance of both work and family in the well-being of the home. He needs to assure his wife of his love, of the dignity of her life, and of her importance to him, while considering what controls he can impose on himself and his time as family breadwinner. "By night on my bed I sought him whom my soul loveth: I sought him, but I found him not" is the sad cry of many a woman today lamenting what draws her husband's attention from herself and their home (Song 3:1). She may, like him, have missed affection from her own parents. Among four things that trouble the earth according to Solomon, burdens whose weight it cannot bear, is "an unloved woman when she gets a husband" (Prov. 30:23, NASB).

The considerate husband does indeed have a balancing act. His wife, as the primary caregiver, is the custodian of family interests and naturally sees family life from her center. Whereas she relates the family to itself as her primary duty, he relates the family both to itself and to the world beyond. She may need reminding that family interests are being served by his attention to concerns beyond the family, concerns that to her may seem less pressing than the immediate ones of the home. Every family, wrote C. S. Lewis, needs a Secretary of State.

A caring father in vocational Christian work may feel hard-pressed to satisfy the counter-pulls of family and ministry. Especially if the children are young, both commitments may exert what seem to him absolute claims upon his attention. Must ministry revolve around family, or must family revolve around ministry? This apparent conflict of obligations may seem an insoluble problem. Keeping family and ministry in equilibrium may seem not to do justice to either.

After years of wrestling with this question, I arrived at what for me has been a satisfying answer. It draws on a planetary analogy. Neither family nor ministry orbits the other. Both orbit the Son. Both orbits, like the earth's, are elliptical, not circular. At times ministry must swing out to allow family to come in closer. At other times family must momentarily swing out in the interests of ministry. But with prayerful discretion the two can orbit without disadvantage to either. In fact their motions can balance each other elegantly in a mutually enhancing way.

The wise Christian father understands that duties on either side of his balancing act can be overpaid. He may have to rule against staying home during a weekend of special services even though Friday night has been designated a family night. Or if he believes church expectations have become excessive, he may decide that the family cannot be kept from home by church activities four or five nights a week. He knows better than to give precedence to either family or church at every point at which their interests compete.

In all this there is a caution for a woman whose husband is in a ministry that makes unusual demands on the family. A pastor or teacher in a Christian institution, let us say, who sincerely does his best to shield his family from the pressures of his work is especially vulnerable to a barrage of complaints from his marriage partner. If she cannot affirm his ministry and encourage him in the life God has given him, the result will not be a happy one. God holds the man responsible for his leadership of the home. He must be considerate and wise. God also holds the woman responsible for the power she can have over the man. If he is tender toward her and sensitive to her criticisms, she can keep him in a conflicted state.

There are other situations in which the biblical division of responsibility in the family can come under special stress. In two-income families there is a natural tendency for the wage earner to claim a right to family decision-making proportional to the share of the income he or she supplies. If the wife works a public job and especially, as is common in two-income ministry families, if she earns more than he does, she may expect an enlarged role in family decisions. Her husband, regretting she has to work, may be inclined to give it to her. A godly discerning wife will not allow this to happen. She shares his vision of their lives. Even if her husband has lost his job or is disabled, she will insist that the biblical family order remain in place—that his impairment not affect his responsibility to lead.

An unforeseen stress may happen when the first child enters the family. Each spouse up to this time has put the other first, and biblically so. Now because of the needs of the baby, priorities can be painfully tested. A husband can become insecure and hurt when he must share the attention of his wife, when her interests seem to fixate on the little one born to them. If the husband feels marginalized, tensions can rise. In wise marriages an adjustment occurs in which each spouse continues to put the other first as before, but in which father and mother *together* subject their interests to those of the child. It is ultimately in the child's interests that neither husband nor wife be neglected by the other. Each still needs the earnest attention of the other. Their little one needs the earnest attention of them both.

An understandable but still serious test of the family order occurs when a flawed husband, conscious of his faults, cedes his God-required leadership to his nobler wife. He regards her as his superior in judgment and character, and perhaps as someone to whom he owes a debt. Because of his past failings, he has lost the moral high ground of leadership, he thinks. His wife may in fact agree and take up his vacated leadership. This reversal of roles would be a serious mistake on both parts. Family authority is God's and his to whom God gives it. "The gifts and calling of God," said Paul, "are without repentance" (Rom. 11:29).

I remember once talking with my father about a friend who had had an affair that nearly broke his marriage but who was able to see the marriage restored. He repented of his infidelity and his wife took him back. Though devastated, she was unwilling for the marriage to end. I was delighted at this answer to many prayers. "She has him under her thumb," I said. "That's wrong," said Dad. "God still expects him to lead." In God's view, the leadership of the family remains with the husband whether he feels worthy of it or not. A wife's response to her demoralized husband should be a simple one. "Obey the Lord."

A father in a tense situation can become tense and short until the moment has passed. Some tolerance is due him. We hear of the pilot of an airliner losing engine power turning his plane toward the nearest airport, or an open field, concentrating all his powers on bringing the plane to a safe landing. His mind is clenched to his business, all he has learned in training and experience riveted to it, as he struggles to save the plane with the lives of those on board. He may snap commands to the passengers and crew expecting instant, complete obedience. He has no time for artful persuasion, for styling his orders agreeably.

Will his passengers and crew be offended by his curt manner? Will they be put off by what might be construed a dictatorial moment? Will they grumble "Who does he think he is? That's no way to handle me!"? Of course not. They fear for their safety. Their lives rest in his hands. Their instant obedience is their best chance to survive.

Tense moments pass, for the pilot and for the head of the home, but Christian fathers live with the knowledge that their families remain under attack by the enemy of their souls. They know that our "adversary, the devil, as a roaring lion, walketh about, seeking whom he may devour" (1 Peter 5:8). Both father and mother (the pilot of an airliner has a copilot) must stay "sober and vigilant" in both storm and calm for the family's safety. It is true that the challenge of a storm does not justify caustic, demeaning words from the captain of the airship. His self-possession will steady the passengers and crew, improving their chances of a safe landing. But his stiff concentration in tight situations shows his care for those he commands.

Pressure has a tendency to isolate a person, and there is no pressure weightier than what is felt by the leader of an enterprise in danger. He will learn very soon and very well if he hasn't already what has been called the loneliness of command. The conduct of a family is a great enterprise. Some of its stresses are inescapable. A father's command, his captain's duty, need not be made lonelier than his role requires.

CHAPTER 10

# BREACHES IN THE WALLS

*When the enemy shall come in like a flood, the Spirit
of the Lord shall lift up a standard against him.*
ISAIAH 59:19

When the Babylonians attacked Jerusalem in 586 BC, they broke through on the north of the city where the wall was lowest, about twelve feet high, ignoring the sides whose walls rose above deep valleys. Since the northern wall was closest to the temple, the attack must have had special psychological impact. Similarly when Satan assaults a family he targets its weakest relationships or those most important to its spiritual strength.

The husband and wife relationship is the preferred target of our great enemy for the reason that everything else in the family depends upon it. Children learn submission from their mother's submission to their father. They learn responsibility from their father's gracious governance of the family. They feel secure in their life world when the family order is stable and assured. When parents tear down each other in the presence of their child—when emotional disagreements are not kept "off-stage"—little may they realize the cost to their authority in the family and the evil harvest their child will reap from their absence of control. As cobelligerents both lose credibility with the child as parental guide. They also may lose respect in their own eyes and tragically back off on their child's discipline, feeling the incongruity of enforcing conduct they have not manifested themselves. No one wins in a parental quarrel—no one, that is, except the enemy of our souls.

Godly couples have learned there is an alternative to responding in kind. When a husband, let us say, feels that a remark by his wife is unjust and wounding, he need not render railing for railing (1 Peter 3:9). He can, instead of snapping back, silently show his disappointment until, at an opportune time, he lets her know he was hurt but has tried to understand what might have caused her to feel that way and what he might do now to help the problem. If she has a Christian heart, she will be moved by his response and perhaps shamed.

If a wife is hurt by cutting words from her husband, she can respond in a similar way—that she is trying to understand why he might feel that way toward her, and that, yes, it would have been helpful to be kindly corrected where she was wrong and not crushed, but that she will take to heart his words nonetheless. If he has a manly heart, he will be moved and even shamed by what she says. No member of a family, after a sharp exchange, should be left wounded by the wayside, feeling hopeless and despised. In the absence of apology and reconciliation the injured spouse or child may settle into dejection and over time resign himself or herself to a failed life.

Often outbursts are not just momentary lapses correctable by a soft reply but eruptions of unresolved hurts and disappointments. They pop up like scattered islands in an archipelago, jutting from their base in an immense volcanic range. The long history of the clashes will be well-known to both husband and wife, though framed differently by each. Precisely how it all started may be long forgotten. Now calm discussion is impossible. Parties talk at each other, not to each other, never with each other. How sad it is when a deep marital divide, a veritable Marianas Trench, has opened from a fault line capable of correction.

Clearly husband and wife must find an occasion for prayerful self-inquiry. Is this the life they want for themselves? Is this the legacy they want for their children? Might they recall a time before the disappointments with each other took hold? Might they discover even yet the foundation stones of their marriage in that mutual self-surrender that came gradually in courtship and was declared at the marriage altar? God can help them if the will is there.

Good things will come of it. A renewal of their love will ripple through their family in a healing way. Kindness after all is catching. A daughter heard her father mumble to himself that they were out of orange juice for breakfast the next morning. Later that day each went to the grocery store unbeknownst to the other. The daughter returned with what her father liked, high-pulp orange juice; he returned with what she liked, juice pulp-free. Both got what they liked—in orange juice and in love.

Sadly such initiatives of love are not always followed by so gratifying a response. There is no guarantee that everyone in a Christian family will be won by loving example. Satan targets all members of the home. As children grow, alienation can grow toward their families, provoked or unprovoked. Sullen foot dragging can break out in open defiance. The walls tremble. Joy takes flight and anger builds toward the disrupters of family peace. Parents blame each other. Children blame parents. Siblings blame each other too. Old times are gone, it seems, forever.

Let us be aware there may be more to the mind of a child than what shows when he vents his wrath. Times of reflection, of self-disappointment and confusion, and even moments of self-loathing may follow. He may realize the damage he is causing to those that matter to him or ought to matter. It has been well said that little does a child realize the extent to which he holds the emotional health of his parents in his hands.

Children have a God-instilled desire to do for themselves and to be themselves. This desire grows from the earliest years, and discerning parents respect it. They are preparing their children to be independent of their direction and guidance, not dependent forever. Satan tries to capture a child's natural impulse toward independence and turn it to the child's and his parents' grief.

Wise parents seek opportunities to assure their child they have no intention of keeping him home forever—that they have an exit plan for him, a plan respectful of his desires and interests, one far better than what he may devise for himself.

Whereas parents of a self-destructing child must take his behavior seriously and will feel it painfully, they can take it too personally. They naturally grieve for what he is doing to himself. So God grieved for His people Israel who rejected the Source of their happiness. Discerning parents understand that beneath their child's defiance is the urgent need of his soul. Their wounding will end when their child's self-wounding ends.

Their anger will end then too. They realize that at bottom his resistance to their authority was his rejection of God. "Against thee, thee only, have I sinned," prayed the fallen David (Ps. 51:4). God promises not to remember our confessed sins. "He will not always chide: neither will he keep his anger forever" (Ps. 103:9). The prodigal's father in Luke 15 is a picture of God. The father in the parable is there for every parent's benefit. The child who has wandered from a parent's love has a waiting friend. Where would any of us be without the unconditional love of God?

A breach in a Christian home is even more distressing when the rogue behavior is that of a parent. It has become all too common among professing Christians for a spouse to renounce all God has wrought in years of marriage and child-raising for a wider world. "He brake the bonds, and was driven of the devil into the wilderness," writes Luke of the demon-driven man (Luke 8:24). "The rebellious dwell in a dry land," says the psalmist (Ps. 68:6). When a spouse leaves, the breach in the family has reached the foundation. The remaining parent must look to God to shore up the tottering structure. Children will need reassurance as amazement and grief leave them languishing in confusion and dejection.

Here is a state of affairs needing immediate heroic action. The suffering of the children, not to mention the victimized spouse, is immense. The sorrow can be world-changing especially for the child closely attached to the sinning parent. In Isaiah 50:1 the

Lord challenges Israel to show just cause for their rejection of Him. He speaks as a father alienated from his children. "Where is the bill of your mother's divorcement, whom I have put away? Or which of my creditors is it to whom I have sold you?" (Isa. 50:1). Implied in this comparison is the terrible pain of a broken marriage for the children. "What grounds do you have for rejecting me?" He asks. "I haven't divorced your mother. I haven't sold you into slavery to pay off my debts. Why are you treating Me as if I have wounded you in this way?" Divorce and enslavement to strangers are co-ranked as understandable causes of child rebellion.

Sometimes, despite the best a parent can do, the walls start to bow and totter. So what then can be done? What can be done, what must always be done, is to strengthen what's left. Is a child in open rebellion? Firm up the center of the family, you and your spouse, and solidify the other children. "There is hope . . . that thy children shall come again to their own border" (Jer. 31:17). Is the transgressor a spouse? Then you, the remaining parent, are now the center. Gather the children, do your best to comfort them, and fasten down their loyalty to God. Keep their spirits hopeful. Teach them by example to overcome anger with love. "Charity hopeth all things, endureth all things" (1 Cor. 13:7).

Is there only one person, you yourself, who still cares about the family enough to rebuild it? Are you left alone? There is still work to do. You are now the center, indeed the entire center and circumference. Firm up yourself and hold steady. "I will walk within my house with a perfect heart," wrote the psalmist David, a lonely figure whose family must have seemed at times to be disintegrating around him (Ps. 101:2).

Keep standards in place. The wanderer will need coordinates to plot his position. He will need landmarks to find his way back. His recovery depends upon your continuance in what you have taught him. When the prodigal son returned, he found his father where he had left him and his home where it was before.

Is there spirit enough to pray? Then pray with the confidence that God can engage the most stubborn minds at any time and in any place. Be assured that His words can penetrate where yours cannot. "Thou holdest mine eyes waking," said the psalmist; "I am so troubled that I cannot speak" (Ps. 77:4). God's words to the sinner are elegantly attuned to their purpose when ours are not. They do not fall idly to the ground.

So take heart. We need not yield to despair until God does. "I the Lord build the ruined places, and plant that that was desolate," said the Lord through His prophet to dejected Israel (Ezek. 36:36). If the walls need rebuilding from very far down, never forget there will be more than one of you busy in the work. The Lord assured us He would be with us "alway, even unto the end of the world" (Matt. 28:20).

# CHAPTER 11

# CHRIST THE DIVIDER

*Think not that I am come to send peace on earth: I
came not to send peace, but a sword.*
MATTHEW 10:34

Chapters 9 and 10 dealt with the grief that can come to a
Christian home from the resistance of a spouse or a child
to the rule of God. Families can also suffer from the obedience
of one of its members to God's rule. Both disobedience to God
and obedience to God can disrupt family unity. Division in a
Christian home because of rebellious attitudes and behavior is
regrettable and destructive. Division in a non-Christian home
resulting from a serious commitment to Christ can be necessary
and constructive.

We may need to adjust our thinking about the importance
of family peace. It is true that the rule of God, in a family or
a person, brings peace. It is also true that where God's rule is
resisted there can be no peace. So are parents or children or siblings who wish to honor God and obey His rule in spiritually
resistant families caught between contradictory commitments?
What needs to be recognized is that family harmony, as natural
and desirable as it is, cannot be the first priority of a home. The
deep unity of a family is rooted in obedience to God, and obedience to God, no less than disobedience, can tear a family apart.

In his first epistle the apostle John refers to disorder in the first family. He makes clear that this disorder did not result from a misunderstanding of family roles or from an unwillingness to abide by them. Cain's insolent reply to God, "Am I my brother's keeper?" was not an expression of honest ignorance concerning how brothers should care about each other. Cain, says John, "slew his brother because his own works were evil, and his brother's were righteous" (1 John 3:12). Cain hated his brother from his being's core because his brother cared about God and Cain did not. God's rejection of Cain's sacrifice sparked Cain's revulsion toward his brother's goodness into a murderous act.

In Luke 12:51–53 the Lord warns that families can be split apart by His call to discipleship. The strongest of natural ties, those of maternal, paternal, filial, and even spousal love, will prove flimsy when tested by Christ's claims on a life.

> Suppose ye that I am come to give peace on earth? I tell you,
> Nay; but rather division. For from henceforth there shall be
> five in one house divided, three against two, and two against
> three. The father shall be divided against the son, and the
> son against the father; the mother against the daughter, and
> the daughter against the mother; the mother in law against
> her daughter in law, and the daughter in law against her
> mother in law.

Jesus is saying that there is a question of personal allegiance whose answer is more determining than the strongest of human ties. This question of allegiance arises in response to His claim of ownership over a life. Response to this claim will be overmastering. Of the slain followers of Christ standing before His throne in Revelation 12:11 it is written, "They loved not their lives unto the death." The impact of their fierce resolve to Christ's call helps us understand why Jesus said He came to divide families rather than unite them.

The divisions mentioned by the Lord in this passage are breaches of loyalty between parent and child. What can be more intimate and fundamental in human life than the biological feelings existing from birth between father and son, mother and daughter? Yet there is a conviction of belongingness deeper than biological identity. It is clear from Matthew 10:36 that Jesus' warning in the passage just quoted was meant to embrace all family relationships. "A man's foes shall be they of his own household."

It is hard to imagine an emotional pain worse than losing a loved family because of a personal choice unless it is the pain of a family from having lost a loved member from such a choice. Jesus' mother was warned by old Simeon, when she came to present her newborn at the temple, that the child would cause her great pain. "Yea, a sword shall pierce through thy own soul also" (Luke 2:35). Twelve years later when His frightened parents found Him in the temple after missing Him for three days, Jesus responded firmly to their chiding: "Wist ye not that I must be about my father's business?" (Luke 2:49).

This exchange would not be the only time, as we saw in chapter 3, when Jesus rejected His family's interference in His developing ministry. There is ample indication in the Gospels of Jesus' affectionate concern for His earthly mother and family. But when their sense of His life clashed with His own, there could be no hesitation. His Father's purpose had to prevail.

When obedience to God must be chosen over family attachments, the pain can be wrenching. We read of Jeremiah's relatives and home community warning him, "Prophesy not in the name of the Lord, that thou die not by our hand" (Jer. 11:21). The Lord replied to His dismayed prophet, in effect, "Family rejection has happened to Me too." "Mine heritage is unto me as a lion in the forest; it crieth out against me" (Jer. 12:8). We read in the opening chapter of John's Gospel, "He came unto His own, and His own received Him not" (John 1:11).

The Lord impressed on His disciples that they should expect no better treatment than He had received. "Remember the word that I said unto you, The servant is not greater than his lord. If they have persecuted me, they will also persecute you; if they have kept my saying, they will keep yours also. But all these things will they do unto you for my name's sake, because they know not him that sent me" (John 15:20–21).

When members of my family turn on me because of my announced commitment to Christ, when their sense of who basically they are, their core identity, drives out their natural feelings toward me, when something so rooted as family love and loyalty is overwhelmed by hatred and contempt, the shock can be numbing, something I could never have imagined, much less prepared for. I may wonder what passion could be so strong as to drive them to that?

Scripture speaks of the offense of the gospel. Whereas Christians are "a savour of life unto life" to "them that are saved," they are "a savour of death unto death" to "them that perish" (2 Cor. 2:15–16). Both their overt witness and the quiet testimony of their daily lives are an affront to those near them who do not share their faith. Within even the closest relationships a profound divide can develop between the "children of God" and the "children of wrath," a deep fissure that family identity and family tradition cannot bridge (Rom. 8:16; Eph. 2:3). The gospel, as spoken and as lived, is obnoxious to the world, for it condemns unbelief at its center. A Christian's very presence can remind those without the Lord of their alienation from God and the danger of their lost condition.

This divide can occur also within a Christian family when one member is minded to be a serious Christian and the other members, though saved, are not. Slack believers do not wish to be reminded of their spiritual drift. Vibrant spirituality in the home is an unappreciated assault on their peace. It is a special sorrow when a child of God is isolated from his biological kin when they are also his brethren in Christ.

Since a personal relationship with God raises all other human relationships, a Christian's rejection by his family will be all the more painful. The more he loves his parents, spouse, children, and siblings, the more he will feel his faithfulness to Christ is costing him. He will do his best to retain their love and will continue to love them in the love of Christ, but the pain is ever there. However judiciously he tempers his witness, the most he can expect from them in the short run may be a God-enabled emotional truce.

In New Testament times the gospel was splitting families, and believers needed advice. Questions arose about whether a marriage between a believer and an unbeliever ought to continue. Should a "woman which hath an husband that believeth not" stay with him? it was asked. Paul answered yes. "If he be pleased to dwell with her, let her not leave him." Paul's explanation is encouraging. "For the unbelieving husband is sanctified by the wife, and the unbelieving wife is sanctified by the husband; else were your children unclean; but now are they holy" (1 Cor. 7:13–14). A Christian wife or husband can influence the rest of the family toward conversion. We have an example from Paul's circle of disciples. The mother of Paul's protégé Timothy, though married evidently to a Gentile unbeliever, was still able to raise a child of fervent faith and sterling character.

The church father Augustine in his autobiographical *Confessions* tells a story that supports Paul's advice to wives. Augustine pays tribute to the longsuffering piety of his mother, Monica, who chose to remain with her pagan husband. By her patient submission and godly example through many years of abuse, Patricius finally came to the Savior and became an exemplary Christian. If an unbelieving husband insists on leaving, writes Paul, let him go. But don't leave him if he is willing to live with you in peace.

The division between Jesus and His brothers must have been painful to Him and to His mother, Mary. We read of their taunting Him, challenging Him to go to Jerusalem during the feast of tabernacles and display His powers to the crowds. We can be sure this was not the only instance of their verbal abuse. "Neither did his brethren believe in Him," writes John (7:5). Jesus knew well the pain of family rejection.

But that is not the last we hear of Jesus' brothers. It is encouraging that the first written of the New Testament books (other than possibly Galatians) was by a brother of Jesus. James had come quickly to the fore in the Jerusalem church after the Lord's ascension, and his voice on difficult questions was considered decisive. Written and circulated somewhat later was the short Epistle by James's brother Jude. It should reassure discouraged Christians whose testimony within their families seems of small effect that a witness as strong as the Son of God's to His own siblings could have been so long resisted. It is also encouraging that a resistance to the truth as ingrained as theirs can eventually yield.

One can scarcely think of a more vehement resister of the gospel than the young Pharisee Saul, obsessed with crushing the new faith. "Breathing out threatenings and slaughter against the disciples of the Lord" (Acts 9:1), he secured authority from the high priest to bring bound to Jerusalem any believing Jews he could find in Damascus. Saul had kept the garments of those who martyred Stephen and would later feel complicit in his death. It is well known how the Lord put a stop to his rage, striking him blind on the road to Damascus. What is less well known is a fascinating fact buried in his greetings to his friends at the end of Romans. Among those he mentions are "Andronicus and Junia, my kinsmen, and my fellow prisoners, who are of note among the apostles, who also were in Christ before me" (Rom. 16:7).

Had the gospel found a foothold within Paul's family, among his relatives, before Paul appears in Acts as a persecutor of Christians? Could a knowledge that this pernicious doctrine had made inroads among his very kinfolk have maddened him? Would it not have been a horrendous embarrassment to a proud Jewish family whose son had been taught in the strictest sect of Judaism, instructed by the preeminent rabbi of Judaism, that this detestable doctrine had invaded it? The conversions of Andronicus and Junia must have shaken the family unity to its foundations. Their defection from Judaism could hardly have been unknown to Paul. It must have fired his zeal to exterminate this pestilent sect.

Is it possible to imagine anyone in a family breached by the gospel harder to live with than the hate-driven Saul? People ordinarily become troubled before they turn to God, and people who are deeply troubled about their relationship to God can be hard to live with. If they are battling the voice of God within, they will likely be quarreling with the voice of God without, reaching them through the witness of Christians near them. When a loved one is hateful because of our commitment to Christ, his belligerency can indicate something positive going on within him. Fire flashes when heaven and hell are contending for a soul.

Has there ever been a greater encouragement to a Christian getting heat from his family than this U-turn of the manic Saul? We pray for an instant turnaround of a life headed wrong, and sometimes spiritual change happens that way. Often it does not. God measures time in His own way, sometimes in hours or days, often in months and years. His idea of timeliness can differ from ours.

England's Elizabeth I liked to travel in her kingdom. A royal *progress* was a formal affair requiring elaborate preparation and entailing considerable expense. Even if the queen's venturing was only within London, her procession would pause at predetermined points where she would be ceremonially received by dignitaries, praised with long speeches, and entertained with rich displays. The queen was in no hurry to get where she was going and seemed to enjoy the delays.

Is it not often so with our God? The great King moves deliberately at His own pace. His progress can require of His subjects much waiting. But he proceeds no less majestically in slow increments than by sudden dramatic intervention.

Jesus had been days late, feared the sisters, when he arrived ready to reunite their family, raising their brother from the dead.

# CHAPTER 12

# CHRIST THE RESTORER

*The Lord is there.*

EZEKIEL 48:35

Problems in Christian families, like problems in a Christian life, can get overanalyzed. God's plan for the family is a simple one, described earlier in chapter 4, the shortest of all. Family difficulties arise when His plan is not followed. So would it not have been enough just to present the plan and end the discussion there?

There is value in identifying faulty thinking and examining where it went wrong. That has occupied us for the greater part of the chapters so far. But analysis can be a distraction when diagnosis is simple and the cure is plain, such as obeying God's recipe. Play directors know that to complicate a bad character is to render him sympathetic, and in modern productions that is often done. Psychiatrists have done the same, seeking empathy with wrongdoers at the cost of moral judgment. So while considering the ways humans deviate from God's plan for the family, we must not lose sight of the simple remedy of their problem, a return to that plan.

That being the case, it is possible to overstrategize the cure. When the remedy is simple, the only challenge is the persuasion of the patient. He may need to have the facts of his problem pressed upon him. His counselor may ponder how best to set out those facts and bring them home to him. He may need to spread out some context and separate some threads. But when in the end the problem is shown to be simple and the cure is made clear, the patient has only to act upon what he has been told.

So it is in the present case. Strife in a family of the sort described in these pages has a selfish root. Though it is true that selfishness complicates lives, and that its consequences can stretch on in what seems an endless tangle, Scripture focuses on the cure. The cure of family disorder is obedience of its members to the plan of God.

A fascinating incident in the Gospel of Luke shows the Lord in person calming strife in a godly home. It happened to be a momentary tiff between siblings, but Jesus seized upon its instructive value for His disciples. We too are meant to learn from it.

With quick strokes Luke sets the scene. "A certain woman named Martha received him into her house. And she had a sister called Mary, which also sat at Jesus' feet, and heard his word" (Luke 10:38–39). The sisters Mary and Martha with their brother Lazarus had befriended Jesus when He was in Jerusalem. Their house was in the village of Bethany on the far slope of the Mount of Olives. It seems to have been the nearest thing Jesus had to a home. We read of His resorting there during the days leading up to the crucifixion. In the account from Luke, He is welcomed into the home by Martha.

The incident contrasts the responses of the two sisters to Jesus' visit. Martha "was cumbered about much serving." The language suggests excessive concern with the details of preparation. Martha loved the Lord and wanted Him honored with the best her household could provide. She complained to Him that Mary, who "sat at Jesus' feet, and heard his word," was not helping her get the house ready. Martha expected the Lord to support her complaint. Her attention was on the meal to be served, and her sister's attention, thought Martha, should be there also. The Lord did not follow her script, however. Martha got corrected, kindly but firmly. "Martha, Martha, thou art careful and troubled about many things. But one thing is needful: and Mary hath chosen that good part, which shall not be taken away from her" (Luke 26:41–42).

Let us note in passing that the Lord did not just even out the differences between the sisters so as to restore family peace. He distinguished between who was in the right and who was in the wrong. Mary's activity was better than Martha's. Martha's complaint was without merit. There is a lesson here for parents who assume that there is always some wrong on both sides of a sibling conflict and that therefore judging between parties is unnecessary. When young Moses intervened in a fight between two Israelite slaves, he singled out him that did the wrong: "Wherefore smitest thou thy fellow?" (Exod. 2:13).

Mary understood better than Martha the mind of her Lord. She knew He had come to give rather than just to receive. She realized that what He had to give to her and her sister and their company was more important than anything she and her sister could do for Him, though nothing in His measured words would indicate He was ungrateful for Martha's work. Martha was encumbered with *much* serving.

The Lord's words to Martha compare the "many things" that can occupy us in our efforts to please God with "the one thing needful." The most important thing of all can get overlooked. God recognizes all that is done for Him. Even "a cup of cold water" given in His name will not be without its reward. Yet surpassing even selfless service are loving Him and attending to His word.

Jesus took the occasion to rank the sisters' activities. His language was not dismissive of Martha's activity. There is work to be done in entertaining Jesus, and Martha was busy in her hostess role. She was fussing over significant details, no doubt, while fussing also with Mary. But Mary's was "the better part." Martha's part was less good. It existed for the sake of Mary's. Here is a lesson for us. There is an activity even more important than Martha's for entertaining Jesus. To accommodate Jesus is to accommodate what is most on His mind to do.

Mary had chosen the part of a learner. During weekdays, boys of a Jewish village would come to the synagogue to be taught at the feet of the local rabbi. They would take their places on the floor sitting in rapt attention, riveted on what he had to tell them. To them he was both mentor and father. Mary knew she was in the presence of the greatest of all rabbis, Jesus the divine Messiah. "She sat at his feet, and heard his words." She prized the moment and had disposed herself to benefit to the fullest.

Martha's part was only preparatory to Mary's part, and it could wrongly impinge upon it. But both parts had their place and still do. Martha welcomed Jesus into her house and, we may suppose, placed Him prominently. Mary sat at His feet hearing His words. Martha received Jesus into the house; Mary received *from* Jesus as His student. Martha accorded Him entrance. She made her house His home. Mary accorded Him attention. She made the home a synagogue.

To welcome the Lord into the fellowship of a family, giving Him the principal place and attending to His words, marks the truly Christian home. It is also the first step and often the only step in the solution of its problems.

# DREAMS

CHAPTER 13

# DREAMING IN THE RIGHT DIRECTION

*And Isaac went out to meditate in the field at the*
*eventide; and he lifted up his eyes, and saw, and,*
*behold, the camels were coming.*
GENESIS 25:63

So far, our discussion of what holds Christian families together and what pulls them apart has centered on families
already or soon to be in existence. But new families begin to
form even before courtship years, and that stage may well be the
most important of all. Homes are being imagined into existence
years before a young man and woman meet each other and start
to think about spending their lives together.

Well before his dating years, a maturing child envisions a
marriage and family of his own, wondering what they might be
like and ought to be like. I call this the dreaming stage. This stage
can be blessed by God as much as any other. In fact, I would go
so far as to say that the success of a marriage can depend on it.
Nothing is more important to the flowering of a marriage than
early imagining in the will of God. Let's call it dreaming in the
right direction.

Successful enterprises begin with mind states in which imagining is coupled with intense desire. Because Satan is masterful
in capturing this dreaming process and perverting it, romantic

envisioning is sometimes seen only as a threat to spiritual stability. This is unfortunate. Imagination and feeling were created into us by God and are meant to flourish in joyous human love. They are wonderfully present in Scripture, most extravagantly in the Song of Songs. In this remarkable series of love songs, lovers' yearning and dreaming are not only celebrated for their own sake but also furnish an imaginative vehicle, both chaste and frank, for the Lord's love of His people. That lovers' yearning and dreaming can be so easily debased speaks to their correspondent power for good as well as for evil.

Western civilization has inherited a moral tradition in which thinking about values is mostly cognitive—a rational sorting out of what is evil and good. This viewpoint rests on Aristotle's definition of man as a rational animal. Someone has suggested another definition of man that separates him equally well from the rest of the animal kingdom. Man, so it goes, is a story-making animal. He can't help making stories, even when he sleeps.

Sigmund Freud, whose theorizing was so subversive of the moral life, nevertheless was not far from right when he observed that the mind has a facility, constantly in use, of embodying wishful thinking in made-up stories. He noted that both when sleeping and when daydreaming, we stage scenarios and set them in motion. Making up stories is an important part of our humanity. While dreaming we are testing purposes as well as dealing with our desires and fears.

It should not surprise us that while Scripture warns against wicked imaginations of the heart it also records instances of God's engaging minds in dreams. God still uses dreams to show us ourselves—to reveal what He wants us to think about. Dreams can bring us to praise or to prayer. They can put us in motion or on our knees. They can push our lives in bad or good directions.

Wise parents are custodians of their child's imagination. They set his imaginative landscape early in life, stocking it with stories from the Bible and other worthy reading. Every child maps his world in his mind, constantly revising its contents. It is the field of his adventuring. It extends vastly from his bedroom door.

He will never cease mapping it—its past, present, and future. Childhood, someone wittily observed, is a branch of cartography. A well-formed imagination is one of the greatest gifts a parent can bestow on a child.

It could be instructive for parents sometime when the house is empty to step into their child's room and settle themselves for a while and try to imagine what their child sees of the home and the world from his bedroom door. Children could benefit from doing the same, stationing their outlook from within their parents' room and imagining how the world of the home might extend from it.

A noted biblical commentator of the last century, George Campbell Morgan, saw value in a lively imagination for biblical interpretation. To understand the Lord's intention in a particular incident, one should, said Morgan, stage the scene in his mind and take his place in the listening crowd. The Pharisees and scribes were listening to Jesus' discourse in Luke 15 on the lost sheep, the lost coin, and the lost son. They were obsessed with sheep and with money—with material wealth. They cared less than they should for lost sons. They despised the publicans and sinners, the outcasts of society who "drew near to hear him" (Luke 15:1). We learn from the incident that God cares about loss. He cares particularly about lost persons. He seeks such and rejoices when they are found. This great gospel truth is vitalized for us by our imagined location in the crowd.

The imagination also comes into play in the Christian's interpretation of his own life. In Scripture, pattern situations provide templates for self-evaluation. Would the reader have stayed with Gideon while the Midianites were blanketing the plain, or would he have been one of the fearful that were sent away? Would he have understood what Jesus meant when He spoke of the leaven of the Pharisees or would he have been dull of hearing like the disciples? Would he have stood with Paul at his defense before Nero or would he have been one of those whose courage failed them? Seeing oneself in Scripture is second in importance only to seeing Christ there.

Among the poetical additions to the biblical story in Milton's *Paradise Lost* is one that pertains to the creation of Eve. We are told in Genesis that God caused a deep sleep to fall upon Adam, during which He removed a rib from Adam's side and formed Eve. In Milton's account, while Adam slept he dreamed. He saw in his dream the extraction of his rib, and then there appeared an amazing creature the likes of which he had never seen or could ever have conceived. She was "so lovely fair, / That what seem'd fair in all the world, seem'd now / Mean, or in her summ'd up, in her contain'd." Adam awakes disconsolate, his vision gone, only to "behold her, not far off, / Such as I saw her in my dream, adorn'd / With what all Earth or Heaven could bestow / To make her amiable." He is stunned. "On she came, / Led by her Heav'nly Maker, though unseen. . . . Grace was in all her steps, Heav'n in her Eye, / In every gesture dignity and love" (*Paradise Lost*, 8.471-89). Adam dreamed of Eve and awoke to find her there. His dream had materialized into reality.

Setting aside its dubious historicity, we can find in Milton's poetical addition to the biblical story a profound psychological truth. In the wisdom of God we dream in the direction of what He desires to give us. We bend our thinking toward the realization of that dream, and our behavior follows. Over time the dream gets refined, but eventually, after some misidentifications, we come upon a figure or scenario that does seem to fit the place in our imagined narrative intended for it. If the dream has been guided by God, its materialization will be joyous and sure.

Such is the story of a young man who since childhood has envisioned himself in a God-blessed life behind a pulpit or on a mission field. He prayerfully chooses a Christian college that can help him realize his dream. Faculty guide his academic choices and challenge his discretionary time. His sense of vocation is converging on a yet undescried divine plan.

Such is the story of a teen, perhaps the same young man, who dreams of meeting the love of his life, a girl with everything to be desired who will share his life, bear his children, and be his closest friend. He cherishes the belief that if he keeps dreaming in the right direction he will in time awake like Adam and find his Eve in the place reserved for her in his dream. She will have been dreaming too.

Dreaming toward purposes is what everyone does whose life will amount to much of anything. It is the start of all great enterprises. But since it is the forming of families that concerns us here, we will settle on the last instance mentioned, the yearning and dreaming that bring a man and a woman together for life. I want to emphasize the inevitability of their dreaming. A young man and woman will be dreaming, about love as about other things, whether they mean to or not. There is no way they will not be dreaming. It belongs to their humanity to dream, and especially is that so in youth.

I want to stress even more the necessity of their dreaming rightly. How they dream will have much to do with their personal happiness. It will have everything to do with the happiness of their future homes.

# CHAPTER 14

# THE SCAFFOLDING

*And he dreamed, and behold a ladder set up on the
earth, and the top of it reached to heaven.*
GENESIS 28:12

All that was said in Chapter 1 of maintaining connections
with parents especially applies in the years of threshold
adulthood when finding a life partner seems to take on special
urgency. When a girl reaches her teen years, she can expect to be
tested as never before to pull back from her parents' standards.
Dating opportunities will not likely come so readily to her as to
the boys, and she may feel she has to take quick advantage of
those that come her way.

But boys also can fixate on a dating interest and throw parental advice to the winds. Giddiness is no respecter of gender.
There is no time when young men and women are in greater
need of the wisdom of their parents than they are during their
dating years, and sadly no time when they are more likely to dispense with it. A famous British playwright once remarked that at
the time a young man needs most to be rational he is most likely
to be a fool. Such sadly is often the case. Still Bernard Shaw's
disdainful view of romance is not the right one for a Christian.

Young persons must decide with themselves in their pre-teen
years, well before they are tested by these powerful desires and
pressing opportunities, to continue relying on the guidance of

their parents. Home standards and rules have been in their interest. Boundaries have served the persons they are to become and the families they will form if God so wills. They must settle with themselves long in advance that certain questions will need to be answered satisfactorily before any love interest can go forward. Let us call these necessary answers the **objectivities** of decision making. In terms of our ongoing metaphor, we can think of them as the scaffolding of constructive dreaming. Dreaming needs a framework to hold it in place until it reaches its consummation.

The first of these objectivities has to do with core identity. A young person who has accepted Christ as his Savior has been born spiritually into the family of God. Most have not. "Strait is the gate, and narrow is the way, which leadeth unto life, and few there be that find it." So replied the Lord to the disciples' question, "Are there few that be saved?" (Matt. 7:14; Luke 13:23). Few hearers of the gospel respond to the divine call in repentance and faith.

The opening of John's Gospel speaks of the Jewish nation's rejection of the sent Redeemer. "He came unto his own, but his own received him not." So it was also with the Gentiles. Only a few would avail themselves of the saving benefit of His coming. But those who did would be taken into His household. "As many as received him, to them gave he power to become the sons of God, even to them that believe on his name" (John 1:11–12).

What is spoken of here in John's Gospel is not religious identity. It is not membership in a particular branch of Christianity. Church affiliation does not constitute belief in the Savior. The Lord made it clear to the religious professionals of His day and their followers that organized religion can stand in the way of salvation. He said and continued to say that it is those few who have recognized who He is and what He came to do and personally accepted Him as their sinbearing Savior who have been given the "power to become the sons of God" (John 1:12).

It follows that the first question to be confronted by a young man and woman contemplating marriage is whether both belong to the same spiritual family. They of course cannot be of the same biological family. Law and custom forbid it. They must, if they intend a truly Christian marriage, be of the same spiritual family. They must both be of "the household of faith" (Gal. 6:10).

Otherwise there will be confusion. The one will have a sense of obligation the other does not have and does not understand. The one will serve an authority higher than the spouse and family; the other at best will serve the spouse and family and then him- or herself. Furthermore, marital fellowship between a believer and an unbeliever cannot be complete. The two can unite on the physical, intellectual, and emotional levels; they cannot unite on the spiritual level, which for the Christian is the most important level of all.

Beyond spiritual kinship is the question of spiritual earnestness. If both would-be spouses are professing believers, is there in both a genuine commitment to the will of God in all areas of life? Will each have a care for the spiritual life of the other? Will there be a willingness to organize married life around obligations to God as, for example, in regular church attendance and church participation? Will a portion of the family income be reserved for the offering plate? Will there be a care for personal spiritual growth that translates into daily disciplines such as personal and family devotions? Is there a concern about the threat of popular culture to the moral health of the family that will control exposure to media entertainment?

Questions of moral character must be addressed. Is there integrity at the core of the other person? Is there a foundation of honesty for lifelong trust? Do personal goals go beyond material gain? Is a kind, caring spirit in evidence? Is there on both sides a spirit of humble gratitude, each viewing the other as a gift undeserved? The meek will inherit the earth, said the Lord in Matthew 5. They also inherit marriages that last.

Related to moral character is emotional maturity. What is the response to disappointment? Have both learned how to "be angry and sin not" (Eph. 4:26)? Has each seen the other at his worst moments as well as at his best? Is each educable, willing to learn from the other? There will be much to learn from one another, from others, and from God. In these and other objective considerations, more than can be mentioned here, parents are equipped by life and motivated by love to cast shrewd, discerning eyes.

Dreaming in the right direction means envisioning within a framework of biblical standards and practical good sense, such as has been mentioned in these pages. This framework should be permitted to serve as a filter in the search for a spouse. It may seem however from what has been said that only a paragon of virtue, fully matured and sanctified, need apply. That, of course, is an unreasonable expectation. What must be determined is whether the desired young man or woman is self-critical and shows a desire for, and some evidence of, progress.

When Martha and I were dating and our relationship was taking a serious turn, she surprised me one evening with a caution. "Ron, I don't think you really know me very well. I have a selfish streak." I didn't let on there were moments I had suspected as much. At the time I wondered whether her admission of a selfish streak was an honest disclosure of a fault to someone she deeply cared about or an extremely clever piece of negative psychology. Or could it be both?

Looking back I can see that it was a test. She needed to see whether I would be satisfied with a flesh-and-blood woman and not the goddess-saint of my imagination. I was to marry a woman conscious of her frailties who was willing to be honest about them to her possible hurt and to grow.

# CHAPTER 15

# THE MYSTERY

*And while he yet spake with them,*
*Rachel came with her father's sheep.*

GENESIS 29:9

If parents are honest with themselves, harking back to their own courting days, they will not minimize **subjectivities** of choice. These are the indefinables partially responsible for the success or unsuccess of offered love. When the objective requirements have been satisfied, subjective considerations come properly into play. Though they do not have the absoluteness of objective standards, or the same status as predictables, they still have their part in the strange business of choice in love. By respecting the subjectivities while insisting on the objectivities, parents connect with the heart of their child.

In a romantic comedy of Shakespeare, a young duke, admirable in every respect, has been wooing a countess within his dukedom to no effect. He can offer her all she can conceivably desire in wealth, position, virtuous character, and love. He, by the way, is a hopeless romantic, full of poetry and groaning. Olivia will not see the handsome young duke. Why? "I cannot love him" (*Twelfth Night*, 1.5.254). And that is that. The objectivities are absolutely satisfied. The subjectivities are not. To a lover they must be satisfied too.

In another romantic comedy Shakespeare has two young noblemen equally earnest and at swords for the love of the same girl. Her father favors the one she disfavors—for no evident reason other than his arbitrary will. Shakespeare is at pains to make the two suitors virtually indistinguishable, in character, temperament, and all things desirable. They are usually costumed the same. And yet Hermia will not budge. "I would my father saw but with my eyes" (*A Midsummer Night's Dream*, 1.1.57). There is no way to justify logically the difference she sees between the two identically drawn gentlemen.

Romeo thought he loved Rosalind before he met Juliet. After that it was only Juliet. Love and infatuation had begun in the same way, at first sight, but infatuation with Rosalind didn't last. Rosalind seems to know from the start that what Romeo thinks is genuine love may be only delusional. Typically in Shakespearean courtship the woman has the cooler head and rebuffs the initial overtures of her lover. She knows she has more to lose if he proves faithless. She must test the young man and put difficulties in his way so that he as well as she can be sure that his interest in her is not superficial.

This whole process by which lovers are attracted to each other, tentatively approach each other, and form enduring bonds is for Shakespeare most fascinating and of heavenly origin. We also should regard it so. God uses romantic attraction to form lasting unions. Initial bedazzlement, captivation, tumultuous stirring, can be comical to the spectator but are not to be disdained. They can lead, as Shakespeare puts it in the words of Hippolyta to the cynical duke, "to something of great constancy" (*A Midsummer Night's Dream* 5.1.27).

Jacob fell for Rachel at first sight and his desire for her proved rooted. He "served seven years for Rachel; and they seemed unto him but a few days, for the love he had to her" (Gen. 29:20). The ardent passion of the lovers in the Song of Songs is romantic feeling at the highest pitch. The lovers idealize each other in high romantic terms. Poetry is at work in their imagining of a coming joyous union. It can hold firm to the end. Ezekiel's wife, soon to be removed from him, is spoken of by God with deep poignancy as "the desire of thine eyes" (Gen. 24:16). Heaven sanctifies the motions of romantic desire in the forming of families it means to bless.

The error of the "in-love" compulsion is, first, the notion that falling in love can happen only once; second, that fervencies so intense are bound to be of God; and third, that if one desires a thing enough he is entitled to it. But romantic feeling is not itself to be blamed for this wrong thinking. Marriage would be poorer without the idealization of the beloved at special times and at all times. God speaks exuberantly of His bride. It is right to be starry eyed while your feet are planted on the ground.

Scripture is generous in setting the bounds of choice. Of the portionless daughters of Zelophehad, whose father had died without a male heir, Moses commanded, "Let them marry to whom they think best." Their freedom did have a boundary. "Only to the family of the tribe of their father shall they marry" (Gen. 36:6). But within that boundary they had free exercise of choice. So it was in Paul's advice to widows. A widow is to marry "only in the Lord." But that being so is "at liberty to be married to whom she will" (Num. 7:39). The Mosaic law in Numbers contains "statutes which the Lord commanded Moses between a man and his daughter." They pertain to a daughter "being yet in her youth in her father's house" (Num. 30:16). They are silent thereafter. God's rules may be more generous than they are sometimes taken to be.

It is striking in this regard how many unlikely marriages are blessed of God. Some appear in the line of the Redeemer— January and May marriages such as those of elderly Jacob and young Rachel, aging Boaz and still youthful Ruth, and perhaps even Joseph and Mary of Jesus' family. Obviously in major life decisions all that Scripture has to say about character and virtue, other timeless priorities are to be taken very seriously; but beyond those objectivities, as I have called them, the subjective is given surprising scope.

When dreaming is anchored in conviction and good judgment, good things come of it. The reverse is also true. The same process of envisioning, of fixating on an object, and drawing thoughts and actions in its direction until it becomes a reality, is the age-old path to sin. In the time of the great flood, God looked on the man He had created and saw that "every imagination of the thoughts of his heart was only evil continually" (Gen. 6:5). There is an idolatry of evil desirings for which the imagination supplies images and story lines. Popular culture is Satan's vestibule, holding minds in perpetual, pointless romantic stirrings. God's lovely doorway to marriage can become hell's anteroom. Marriages can founder well beforehand when they are imagined in the wrong way. A natural God-given power can serve as well for evil as for good.

But our principal claim has been the possibility, let us say even the necessity, of constructive dreaming. A Christian home will be dreamt into existence by future homebuilders long before they exchange vows at the marriage altar. Their home-to-be will flourish if they make the Builder of worlds the Lord of their yearnings and imaginings. Few habits are more important in every condition of life than right dreaming for bringing the best of God's blessings to pass.

# CHAPTER 16

# FLAWED EXCELLENCE

*I press toward the mark for the prize*
*of the high calling of God in Christ Jesus.*
PHILIPPIANS 3:14

Scripture records no dreams of Abraham like those of Jacob, Jacob's son Joseph, Daniel, John the apostle, and a number of others. Yet Abraham must be accounted one of the most notable dreamers in sacred record. He sojourned in a land promised to him that was not his, taking possession of it only in his mind. And then, beyond the land of Canaan, which would be settled by his descendants after five hundred years, there beckoned an even more distant habitation, a "city which hath foundations, whose builder and maker is God" (Heb. 11:10). Abraham's imagination bent his life toward an unseen goal.

His partner in dreaming was his wife. While Abraham dreamed of a permanent inheritance, Abraham and Sarah dreamed of a promised succession. But as the decades went by, Sarah's expectation withered and died. Barren years and barren hopes—these seemed the fruit of listening to God. But Abraham's sojourning and Sarah's conceiving are commended to us in Hebrews 11 as supreme instances of godly faith.

This commendation is puzzling because, particularly on Sarah's side, little in Genesis seems to justify it. Before journeying from their homeland Abraham got Sarah's consent to be misidentified as his sister. Sarah was beautiful even in advanced years, and a beautiful woman might be taken by greedy rulers at the cost of her husband's life. Twice God had to force rulers by threat of judgments to give her back. In Genesis 20 Abraham is rebuked for dishonesty and Sarah for immodesty by a Philistine king.

In the part of the narrative in which she mainly appears, it is Sarah who is at the helm, dictating to Abraham, and not wisely. Now in her mid-seventies, she is still barren. Their promised male heir has not appeared. Sarah insists that they take matters into their own hands. They should enable God's promise of heirs by means of a wife surrogate. Hagar, Sarah's proud Egyptian handmaid, a non-Hebrew, would then be the ancestress of a Hebrew nation. Such is the plan Sarah proposes and such the plan with which Abraham complies.

Hagar promptly conceives and can't resist showing glee in Sarah's presence. Barrenness was a shame to a woman in the ancient world, and Hagar cared little for tact in a touchy situation. Sarah, whose name meant "princess," was not about to be lorded over by her handmaid. When the situation turns sour, Sarah blames, of all people, Abraham for letting it happen. "The Lord judge between me and thee," she said (Gen. 16:5). Sarah with Abraham's consent drives out Hagar and her unborn child, and into the desert with Hagar goes Sarah's plan to furnish Abraham an heir.

Thirteen years later God declares to Abraham the time has come for him to have a male heir by Sarah. It comes as a shock. Abraham, now ninety-nine, has grown accustomed to thinking of Ishmael as his heir. He no doubt truly loves him, and his faith hesitates. God curtly repeats the declaration and leaves. It is possible Abraham did not report this encounter to Sarah, fearing her response.

Shortly afterward, three angelic visitors, one of them the Lord, appear at midday at Abraham's tent door unrecognized and are welcomed. The Lord directs a message to Sarah, eavesdropping behind the tent door, reiterating His promise that she will conceive and bear Abraham a son. The birth will happen a year from this time. Sarah laughs within herself at the absurdity and is sharply rebuked for her unbelief. Terrified, she denies having laughed and is again rebuked, now for dishonesty—"Nay; but thou didst laugh" (Gen. 18:15).

The rebuke is necessary. Sarah will have to cooperate right away with her husband to conceive the child so it can be born within the indicated term of a year. She obviously does so. As the results gradually appear in Sarah's aged body over the nine months of her pregnancy, we can be sure that her confidence in God's promises is rebuilding as well. Her faith is being restored.

So is her joy. A year later Isaac—his name means "laughter"—is born, and Sarah laughs again, but not in bitterness. "God hath made me to laugh, so that all that hear will laugh with me. . . . Who would have said unto Abraham, that Sarah should have given children suck? For I have born him a son in his old age" (Gen. 21:7). Sarah will live to see Isaac mature into his thirty-seventh year.

Sarah's family troubles are not over, however. She notices Ishmael mocking her little Isaac and becomes infuriated. She pressures Abraham to rid her of Hagar once again along with her son; and Abraham, grieved but instructed by God to do so, sends them away. God tells Abraham He will take care of Ishmael and make of him also a great nation. In disposing of her rival, Sarah has cleared the path for Isaac's succession to the promised inheritance, though in a regrettably messy way.

What are we to make of this checkered history of Sarah in the light of the tributes accorded her later in Scripture? In Hebrews Sarah has an honored position next to her husband among the great exemplars of faith. "Through faith also Sara herself received strength to conceive seed, and was delivered of a child when she was past age, because she judged him faithful who had promised" (Heb. 11:11). Even more striking is the celebration of Sarah by the apostle Peter in his first epistle as a model of godly wifehood. Peter specifies the inner beauty of "a meek and quiet spirit" as a virtue to be sought by all wives who would emulate Sarah and rise to her standard. Wives can be "daughters of Sarah" if they "do well" and reverence their husbands not from fear but from sincere conviction and love. The bar is set high. "Sara obeyed Abraham, calling him lord" (1 Peter 3:4–6).

This spirited woman, at times contentious, who was compliant when she oughtn't to have been and incompliant when she should have been had something about her that would live on as a pattern to be observed. How might that be? I find here an encouragement for all who feel they have fallen short in the business of family formation. It can be an encouragement to us all.

Something planted deep in Sarah wanted to please her husband and please her husband's God. She deserves some sympathy. She has followed her husband faithfully from location to location without the satisfaction of a settled life. When Abraham heeds God's summons to leave his kindred and go, she must leave her kindred too. She has never known a permanent home and a family life with her own children. All she has heard of a promised heir has come to her through the mind of an aging man. Now in her late eighties for a visitor to raise those withered hopes once again without, for all she knew, any certainty of fulfillment might seem to anyone cruel. And yet, when God addresses her directly at the tent door, she yields at once to her greater Lord and becomes Abraham's partner in fulfilling the promise.

What we find in Sarah and in every striving Christian can be described as a flawed excellence. Sarah had her disappointing moments, one of which must have seemed in hindsight disastrous. She would have much to regret. But God summed her life with as generous a commendation as any could wish for. Despite notable lapses Sarah pressed on in her role as wife and mother and was extolled for it.

# MORE DREAMING

There are stories in the Bible that remain to be discovered, even by readers familiar with the Scriptures for years. One of them is especially interesting to me since it has a claim to being in its way the greatest miracle of all. It has only the briefest mention in Mark's Gospel. It is tucked into the text in a way that makes it easy to miss.

The story is of a man who appears only momentarily and seemingly by accident in the march of events leading to Christ's crucifixion, though we know there are no accidents in the plan of God. Then he drops out of sight. Or does he?

It should strike us as strange that this obscure figure is identified for us in the narrative by name and origin. "And as they came out [from the governor's hall], they found a man of Cyrene, Simon by name: him they compelled to bear his [Jesus'] cross" (Matt. 27:32). Cyrene was a Roman town of North Africa in what is now Libya. It had a large Jewish population estimated at about two hundred thousand. Jews from Cyrene would hear Peter preach at Pentecost. Some became believers and carried the gospel to Antioch (Acts 13:1).

Ordinarily the condemned man was required to bear his own cross. But Jesus was so weakened by the scourging and buffeting He had received that His strength soon gave out. Simon just happened to be there, or so it would have seemed to the onlooking crowd. What a shock, what a humiliation, for a visitor, a proud foreigner. If he was an observant Jew, he had to stay ceremonially clean for the feast. It involved among other things avoiding contact with dead bodies or anything that had to do with them. But the Roman soldiers were all business. They despised such scruples. They "laid hold of him" and "laid the cross" on him. He had to carry on his shoulders the repulsive thing. What a degrading spectacle it must have made of him. What a degrading business was required of him. He would never live it down.

We don't know what motive had brought Simon to Jerusalem. We may assume he was a Jew by belief, since he had a Jewish name and had come to Jerusalem at Passover time. Tradition has it he was a native African, and that seems very possible. Something about him made him stand out from the crowd. From Mark and Luke's accounts, which speak of Simon as "coming out of the country," we may wonder if he hadn't just then entered Jerusalem for the feast, his appearance showing the effects of his journey.

On at least two occasions before His crucifixion Jesus had spoken to His disciples about cross bearing. In His commissioning of the twelve before sending them to cities where He had not yet preached, He warned them, "He that taketh not his cross and followeth after me is not worthy of me" (Matt. 10:38). Later when He informed them to their dismay of His coming treatment by the Jews in Jerusalem, He repeated the warning. "If any man will come after me, let him deny himself, and take up his cross, and follow me" (Matt. 16:24). Now after His disciples have fled, a foreigner is compelled to meet the standard of true discipleship. Though the Cyrenian would not share in Jesus' death itself, he would share in the shame of it.

The incident alone would be an interesting irony if it were all there were to the story. The fact that the cross bearer's name is given by Mark and in two of the other Gospels, suggests there is more to the story. Mark gives an additional detail in his account of the incident. "And they compel one Simon a Cyrenian, who passed by, coming out of the country, the father of Alexander and Rufus, to bear his cross" (Mark 15:21). Mark assumes some knowledge in his readers of the cross bearer and his sons. It seems evident that by the time Mark was writing Simon had become a disciple and so had his sons.

Now we venture into what seems to me a reasonable speculation. One of Simon's sons may be among those greeted by Paul at the end of his epistle to the Romans. "Salute Rufus, chosen in the Lord, and his mother and mine" (Mark 16:13). The expression "chosen in the Lord" may indicate an extraordinary circumstance in his conversion. If this Rufus is the same one referred to by Mark, the woman mentioned as his mother was Simon's wife. She had made herself a mother to Paul. As mothers do, she had brought him under her care and taken charge of his needs, distance permitting. It was a tender reference by Paul. Perhaps an exile from his own family, Paul had found a mother, or rather she had found him and adopted him. She had reenlarged his family connections.

Now, is it not a miracle that this visitor to Jerusalem, forced to shoulder a grotesque instrument of death on behalf of a stranger, later took it up of his own will as a disciple of that stranger? How could such a thing be? How could the involuntary become voluntary in such a revolting matter as this?

There may be readers of these pages who were like Simon "compelled to bear the cross." Oh, I don't mean a heavy wooden crossbeam. I mean something considered no less burdensome and repulsive. You were made to go to church when you didn't care to. On Sunday morning it was Sunday school and then the morning service. On Sunday evening it was another service. There was a midweek service and special services and gatherings at other times. Your social life was centered in the church, perhaps a small church, and was strictly controlled by your parents' standards and rules. You couldn't go to dances, the pop concerts, or the movies your friends were talking about. You couldn't watch the TV programs or listen to the music they listened to and talked about. Perhaps you couldn't watch TV at all. Your parents had dress standards that set you apart from your social peers and marked you as different. You stood out from your surroundings as did Simon that day in Jerusalem.

You may have been sent to a Christian school through twelfth grade or even schooled at home and, if that weren't bad enough, enrolled afterward in a Christian college confined by restrictions similar to those you had known all your life. And the resentment grew. A child restricted by beliefs that are not his own and embarrassed by them can become angry with his parents and their beliefs and with their God. He may pass through his teen years with a deepening grudge.

Fathers have been converted in middle life and changed the course of their families' lives. Husbands called to special Christian service have required sacrifices from their families the children were unprepared for and did not fully accept. Life on a mission field or subsistence in a low-paying ministry at home can be a hard adjustment for a child and even harder for the wife when the family has been better off materially before. Involuntary servitude—cross bearing—is a tiresome, frustrating, wearing thing. It may seem a living martyrdom, if there can exist such a thing.

And yet, the great marvel is that it isn't always that way. In Simon's case at least, the involuntary became voluntary. That would be wonder enough, but the cross, it appears, became voluntary for his family also. Children who honor their father can feel his shame even more keenly than he does. And yet in the sons and also we think in their mother the same transformation occurred. Along with Simon they became known and beloved throughout the Christian world.

Christian parents impose upon their child beliefs and standards that set him apart from the world and make him a spectacle to his peers. He becomes a stranger and pilgrim on earth with his parents without being asked his opinion. Parents pray and dream of what may seem to them at times impossible, that somehow and someday their beliefs will become their child's own. How can a child who feels denied full participation in life because of convictions not his own—how can such a child ever change his mind? How can he change his heart? Easier bring a body from sickness to health, even from death to life, than create a heart of flesh from a heart of stone. And the months and years may go by and the dream may dim.

But it can happen even after long years that what has been imposed becomes embraced, that the involuntary becomes voluntary, that the cross pressing so grievously on the child is taken up willingly and gladly borne. And when it happens—be assured it can happen—it will rank with the greatest miracles of God.